Other Books by Cherise Kelley

Dog Aliens 1
Raffle's Name

Dog Aliens 3
She Wolf Neya (2014)

My Dog Understands English!
50 dogs obey commands they weren't taught

High School Substitute Teacher's Guide
YOU CAN DO THIS!

Dog Aliens 2
Oreo

Cherise Kelley

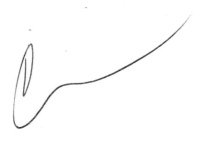

ISBN: 1481923013
ISBN-13: 978-1481923019

Cover Design by Annette Tremblay
www.midnightwhimsydesigns.com

DEDICATION

To Raffle. You're the most obedient dog ever.
To Oreo. I have never felt more protected.

Contents

CHERISE KELLEY

ACKNOWLEDGMENTS

Thank you, Shaun Ellis, for publishing your
experience living with the wolves and allowing the
rest of us to live with them vicariously.

Thank you, Veterinary Vision, for your informative
article, "What Do Dogs and Cats See?"

Thank you, Wolfcountry.net, for your excellent
articles on wolf senses, wolf life span, wolf pack
structure, and how wolves play.

Chapter 1: Raffle

The animal shelter employee pulled the Springer Spaniel / Border Collie mix's speckled lips back so my humans could see that he lacked teeth in the sides of his mouth.

"See? Oreo is just a puppy."

My male human said, "Well, I guess our Queensland Heeler will be helping us raise this Springer Spaniel puppy!"

His mate said, "Can you hold him while we go get him a collar and a leash?"

It wasn't an odd question considering how the animal shelter had ambushed my humans at a Pet Smart store.

They'd gone in to look around at things for me. They hadn't brought me because the trip hadn't been planned. They'd stopped on their way home from the movies. I heard them talking about it later.

When they entered the store, they noticed about 50 kennels near the entrance, with big signs saying "Adopt Me!" Not even a human could have missed the display. I saw it later on that evening.

At first, my humans ignored the homeless animals and went about shopping around for toys and treats for me, as they did every week or so, bless them. They went up and down every aisle in the big-dog section, handling squeaky toys, raw-hides, and even cookies meant for dogs. They never bought any of those silly dog cookies. I prefer dog biscuits. They're healthier.

Gradually, my humans' curiosity about what types of animals the Humane Society had brought to be rescued got the better of them.

"Wanna go check out the animals they brought for adoption from the pound?"

"I thought you'd never ask!"

With big grins on their faces, they rushed over to look. There were a few cats, but the vast majority of the kennels contained abandoned Kaxians. You humans call us 'large breed dogs'.

"We really should get Raffle a girlfriend, to keep him company when one of us can't be with him," she said.

"Or a buddy, anyway," the animal shelter employee interjected.

"Yeah, a buddy would be good."

"Look! This female kind of looks like him."

"Yeah, she kind of does."

"Excuse me, Sir?"

"Yes?"

"Can we see this dog outside her kennel?"

"Sure."

They petted her and tried to play with her, but she was skittish and timid. She barely raised her head up to look them in the eyes. Still, my mistress was hung up on the idea of getting me a girlfriend. She tried really hard to like this skittish, timid dog that looked like me.

My master had another Kaxian in mind to be my buddy, though.

"Let's put her back." He waved at the animal

shelter employee. "Sir! Yeah, we're not interested in this one after all. Thanks." He showed her the dog he had in mind.

The funny thing was that sometime between that moment and when they entered the store, they had gone from buying toys to deciding to rescue another dog! Now it was just a question of which dog they were going to adopt.

The dog my master had in mind for my buddy, and the one my mistress determined would be my new 'baby brother', is a mix between a show-bred English Springer Spaniel and a Border Collie, with more wolf in him than I have. He's all black except for white smatterings on his paws, chin, throat, stomach, and the tip of his tail.

"This one looks like he'll play more than that other one," my male human said. "See how alert he is?"

"Yeah, maybe that other one is old," my female human said.

The animal shelter employee said, "This one is a puppy, so he'll play a lot!"

"He's a puppy? He's so big, though."

"Yeah, see? Look at his teeth."

And this is where we came in, when my female human said, "Can you hold him while we go get him a collar and a leash?"

"Of course. There is some paperwork you need to fill out first, though."

"OK."

They filled out the paperwork, made their adoption of Oreo official, and were halfway through picking out not only a collar and leash but also a harness, a sleeping kennel, a comfy bed, dog dishes, a long-hair dog brush, and a dozen toys—before they started wondering what my reaction might be, to them bringing a strange dog into our home.

"What about Raffle? Won't he try to eat Oreo if we bring him into the house?"

"Oh, yeah. Hm. Maybe it would be better if we brought Raffle here to meet our new puppy."

"Yeah, he's less territorial when he meets other dogs away from home."

They bought all the new stuff, took it over to the Humane Society's display at the front of the pet store, picked up Oreo, and put his new leash and collar on him.

"We need our current dog to meet Oreo before we will be sure we can take him home. My husband is going to get Raffle and bring him here to meet Oreo. I'm pretty sure it will be OK, but we need to do this, just in case."

"Yeah, OK, we understand."

And that was the first time Oreo ran away.

My mistress was sitting in the store with her new 'puppy' and a shopping cart full of stuff for him. I was walking up to the store with my master, to meet my new 'baby brother'.

He slipped out of his collar and ran under some displays to escape down the main aisle of the store, toward the reptile aquariums in the back. My mistress had a shopping cart full of stuff she didn't want to get stolen, so she did the best she could to wheel it in front of her as she chased him through the store displays.

"Excuse me! Coming through! Sorry!"

She jigged and jagged around piles of dog food bags, trying to keep Oreo in sight. Toys fell on the floor and squeaked loudly. All the Kaxians and

Niques in the store barked.

Fortunately, all the other pet store customers were either amused or sympathetic. Unfortunately, none of them did a thing to help. They all just looked at each other and laughed or smiled.

She finally had to leave the cart in the aisle and crawl after her new 'puppy' into a warren of kennels piled up in a corner before she caught the little stinker.

When I first saw Oreo, the two of them had just returned to the front of the store and were panting in their seats by the Humane Society's display.

"You're no puppy!" I said to my new 'baby brother'.

"Aw, relax. If your human wants to treat me like a puppy, then I'm all for it."

She did want to. She was cuddling him protectively. She seemed concerned about us barking at each other, too.

"Be nice, Raffle!"

"Ha ha! You have to be nice to me now!"

"Be nice, Oreo!"

He wasn't going to cooperate, but I quickly composed and sent him a mental movie of the two of us paling around together: barking at the Niques together through our back-yard fence, for one thing, but also just standing next to each other and not being aggressive, here at the store and in the truck on the way home.

Our mistress was happy that we had stopped barking at each other, and she stood between us so she could pet both of us, one with each hand.

Just as we all were leaving together, one of the shelter employees came up to our humans and spoke in a whisper, as if that could keep me or Oreo from hearing him. Silly human.

"What's the kennel for?"

"We crate train. It's a safe place for Oreo to sleep."

"Oh. Well, you may find him more resistant to crate training than most puppies."

"Why's that?"

The shelter employee was still whispering.

"He was abandoned in a crate."

My mistress started crying as she cuddled Oreo and petted him and tried to reassure him he would not be abandoned again.

"Oh my poor, poor puppy. We're going to love you and take care of you and never abandon you. I promise."

My master joined in on petting Oreo, and agreed to the promises his mate made.

"Yes, yes, Boy, yes."

Our humans loaded Oreo's sleeping crate, dishes, and toys into the camper shell of our little truck, put harnesses on us both, and then seat-belted me into the little space behind the passenger seat and Oreo behind the driver seat.

On the way home, they parked at a restaurant. They took us both out for a short walk to do our business and then seat-belted us behind the seats again. It was winter now in the Coachella Valley, so the windows were only cracked open, not wide open like in summer. They went inside the restaurant.

"Forget this. I'm getting out of here!"

Oreo started chewing through the seat-belt in front of him, frustrated about being tied to the truck through his car harness.

"Quit that!"

Oreo laughed.

"Just because she thinks I'm a puppy and she told you to be nice to me, that doesn't mean I'm going to do what you say. Dream on."

He kept on chewing. He wasn't even chewing on the seatbelt that had him tied to the truck, but I wasn't going to point that out.

The one he was chewing kept my master safe while he was driving the truck! I had to stop him, to keep my master safe. I tried playing a mental movie of Oreo going to sleep, but I couldn't get through. His mind was bright lavender with resentment, at me, no doubt. Instead of using a mental movie to control him, I tried to reason with Oreo.

"It's pointless, though! Even if you chew all the way through the seat-belt, you're still locked inside this truck cab!"

But Oreo didn't listen. He kept right on chewing. He was already halfway through.

I tried reason again.

"You won't be able to open the door and get out anyway, so stop!"

Eyes mocking me for being tied up and unable to stop him, he kept chewing. He was almost all the way through when our humans came back. My master was less than pleased.

"Ahhhhhh!"

"What's wrong?" said the calm but resigned voice of our mistress.

"Oreo chewed the seat-belt all up!"

"Oh no!"

My master's mind was a red ball of rage. I hate to think what might have become of my new 'baby

7

brother' if the seat hadn't been between him and my master, but to give him credit, my master stormed on foot into the sage brush and cactus to cool off.

My mistress wisely let her mate go off alone to calm his rage.

When he returned to the truck, I fully expected him to declare we were taking Oreo right back to the animal shelter. I debated playing my master a mental movie to stop that from happening. I would be able to. His mind was a calm blue once more when he got back to the truck.

I did have a duty to protect Oreo and watch out for him. He was a fellow Kaxian, an alien from the planet Kax, just like me. I knew this because all large-breed dogs are Kaxians. Small-breed dogs are from a rival planet called Nique.

But, Oreo was so obnoxious!

I hesitated longer than I am proud to admit. I didn't need to decide, though.

My master aimed the truck toward home. My mistress sighed, and we all kept quiet the rest of the way home, each lost in our own thoughts.

We got home a little while later. It was dark out, and time for me to be fed. Time for Oreo to be fed, too, I guessed. Before unbuckling the ruined seat-belt and letting Oreo out of the truck, our master petted him while he gave him a little lecture. I backed the lecture up with a mental movie.

"Oreo, Puppy, you can't chew seat-belts. No! Now, you aren't going to ride in the car again until we have a muzzle for you, and for the rest of your life, you are going to wear a muzzle whenever you are in the car."

It turned out Oreo was a 'pet-me' type. As soon as

our human started petting him, he rolled over onto his back and exposed his belly to be scratched. Our human obliged gently and with love.

Our mistress stood back smiling, watching her mate pet her new 'puppy'. She spoke with excitement.

"Shall we take him inside and feed them both and then show Oreo around his new home?"

My master's voice was soothing.

"Yeah, Puppy. Come see your new home."

My master carried Oreo's sleeping kennel, comfy bed, dog dishes, long-hair dog brush, and dozen toys inside. My mistress took us both through the gate into the grassy fenced back-yard to do more business on our way into their den.

Our Nique neighbors, Cherry the Chihuahua and Fred the Toy Poodle, came out to chide us through the tall wooden fence, of course. Also of course, they had heard our human lecturing Oreo, and they could smell Oreo's true age for this life, just as I could.

"Ha ha!" Fred said.

"How's it going, three-year-old 'puppy'?" Cherry said.

"I'm glad I don't get muzzled in the car."

For once, I agreed with our Nique neighbors, so this time I didn't send mental movies to the squirrels high up in the pine trees, telling them to pummel the Niques with pine cones. Oreo took it in stride, though. I was beginning to think he had no shame.

"It's going great! I've got two pushover humans to feed me and pet me, and Raffle here has to be nice to me because they said so. Life is good!"

"Well, good luck with the 'puppy' stuff."

"Yeah, your humans have to let you out."

"You don't have a doggy door like we do."

"Ha ha!"

The Niques tried to rile Oreo up, but his mind stayed cool as a cucumber. In spite of all the annoyance I still harbored for my new 'baby brother' because of his lack of respect for our humans, I was impressed at how he avoided being annoyed by the Niques. What he said next exemplified his cavalier attitude toward them.

"Whatever makes you feel good about yourselves."

Just then, our mistress called us in for food, and we took off running for it. Food is good!

After we ate, our humans showed Oreo around the house. First, they showed him our pack's orange carpeted sleeping den with their king-size bed and our two sleeping kennels, mine on our master's side of the bed, and Oreo's on our mistress's side.

"Go in your house, Raffle."

I went inside my sleeping kennel. It's really much more like a wolf den than the big bedroom is. I like it in there. It's my refuge, especially when scary human toddlers visit.

Oreo did not want to go inside his sleeping kennel. We all understood why, but my master was determined.

"Go in your house, Oreo."

Oreo wasn't budging. My master picked him up and put him in his kennel.

"Good boy, Oreo."

As soon as my master let Oreo go, he flew out of the sleeping kennel with a big scowl on his face and started threatening to run away. Of course, I was the only one who could understand what he was saying.

"That's enough of this kennel stuff, and I'm not wearing a muzzle, either. First chance I get, I'm out of here for good."

Next, they took us all the way down the orange carpeted hall to the white-tiled kitchen and showed Oreo where the water was.

"Drink water, Raffle."

I dutifully drank from the water dispenser. As it always does after I drink, the bowl filled, and air bubbles went up into the top of the water dispenser.

Oreo must have never seen a water dispenser before. He jumped three feet at the sound the air bubbles made!

"Wow! He's afraid of the water dispenser, Scott!"

"Get him a bowl of water, then, and let's make sure he knows where he can drink."

She put a bowl of water down next to the water dispenser and ruffled the surface of the water with her hand.

"Oreo, drink water!"

I knew he understood her, but he played dumb, just looking at her with his ears perched up, wagging his tail.

"Raffle, drink water."

This was getting tiring! I dutifully drank again.

"Good boy, Raffle!"

"Oreo! Drink water!"

They did more hand swishing in his water dish.

He played like he finally got it, and at last drank some water.

"Good boy, Oreo!"

Both of our humans beamed smiles at him and petted him.

They might have been fooled, but I wasn't. I let him know, too.

"Why did you have to make that so difficult?"

"It was worth it. I got fresh water, didn't I?"

And then my mistress complicated my world almost beyond belief by making me Oreo's caretaker while she was busy earning money to buy our food and her mate was sleeping so he could do the same.

"Come, Raffle!"

I ran to her, like I always do.

She scratched my belly while I stood next to her, like she always does.

"Look, see how I'm cleaning Oreo's face? See? He has crumbs on his cheeks and eye-snot coming out of his eyes. We need to clean his face for him. Let's clean his ears, too."

She showed me how to clean the "puppy's" ears, and then went on.

"Raffle, Oreo is just a puppy, and we need to take care of him. You will have to care for him while I am busy with my work."

She petted me then, and smiled at me as she sealed my fate by idly giving me a binding command.

"Take care of your baby brother, Raffle. Keep him from running away from me again."

Chapter 2: Lido

Lido the English Bulldog smiled at his mate. Skil the black Labrador Retriever threw her tail up high, perked her ears at him, and then said what she had said every morning for the past year.

"I'll race you to the front gate!"

"OK! 1, 2, 3, go!"

They both took off running.

Lido's belly had gotten much smaller since Skil's humans adopted him from the animal shelter a year ago. These new humans weren't as generous with the food. They assumed their working dogs would hunt. Lido supposed that was a good thing. He could run faster now. Skil still won all their races, but that was OK with him.

He nearly caught up with her. Nearly.

Skil ran past rows and rows of grapevines that were green and bore new fruit. Even though it was winter, this was the desert. It never froze, and the sun was almost always shining. Humans grew food here year-round. The water came through a human-made river that ran for hundreds of miles from the nearest real river, the Colorado, before it delivered the water to pipes that ran underground for miles here to Lido and Skil's humans' vineyard.

Lido ran just behind Skil, not really worried about

passing her, just happy to be with her. Behind her, he could take advantage of the headwind: watch the way it blew through her fur and breathe in her scent, which the wind wafted back to him in a pleasing way.

The vineyard's three Rottweilers—Boss, Betsy, and their son Blackie—were at the front gate as usual to see Lido and Skil off for the day.

"Have a great day defending the mine!" Boss and Betsy called out together.

Lido and Skil smiled at them as they ran by.

As usual, Blackie scowled at Lido and smiled at Skil.

Also as usual, Skil didn't smile back at Blackie.

Lido was glad the pack of working dogs was large enough that neither he nor Skil was ever alone with Blackie. Lido could take care of himself, but he wouldn't want to risk making Boss mad at him. He imagined Boss would take his son Blackie's side if he and Blackie ever really got into a fight.

He also didn't trust Blackie alone with Skil. Especially now.

Lido gave Blackie his best tough guy look as he ran by, and then Lido tried to forget Blackie and go on about his business. He wished Blackie would mind his own business, too.

Oh yeah, he was trying to forget about Blackie.

Blackie was still scowling at him.

Very deliberately, Lido looked the other way.

He could see the pack's three German Shepherds—Poht, Tog, and Gim—and the pack's two Pitt Bulls—Rel and Kesh—out scaring crows away from the new grapes. They raised their noses to Lido when they saw him looking at them. It was their more casual way of saying "Have a good day defending the mine."

Every day, Lido and Skil ran out of the vineyard, up the dirt road, down the grassy parking strip by a treed boulevard, and then along a hill by the freeway, which took them to their pack's territory. They were very careful to look both ways before crossing the streets, of course. In all, they ran twenty-four miles from the vineyard to the edge of town, where their pack mined jex.

As Lido entered the pack's territory, Skil was waiting for him by their first scent pole, a huge pine tree. She was calmly licking her paw and looking up at him with a twinkle in her eyes. Her tail wagged widely, giving away her intent to tease him about how long he took to get there and how much faster she was.

Lido didn't care if she was faster than him. She was beautiful! Besides, she was a retriever. Retrievers are built for running. Each breed has its specialty, and there's no sense resenting the abilities a specialty brings. He felt good about being able to protect his mate if anything dangerous caught up to her.

She play nipped his nose when he finally got there.

He mock growled and play bit her ear, and then they were off running again.

They both stopped at all the scent poles to smell the pack's scent messages, which told them where to go find today's pack mining operation. Same site as yesterday it was, and off running they went, off the very edge of the concrete and into the sagebrush, cactus, rocks, and reddish dirt of the Coachella Valley.

They could smell the pack when they got within a mile of the mine. They could smell the new recruits the pack had to train today.

Skil and Lido were both defenders now that they

were grown-ups. They helped train new recruits. They were happy with their jobs, but knew they would soon stop coming to the mining site, once they had pups of their own. Soon.

Skil wasn't showing yet, but soon all this running would be too hard on her unborn pups, and Boss had already assigned Lido to new duties back at the vineyard, effective soon.

As usual, the two of them were the last to arrive at the mining meeting, down inside the mining cave, but Heg permitted it because they also traveled the farthest.

Koog was addressing the 9 pack members and four new puppy recruits.

"…OK, they're here! Great. Lido and Skil, Jal and Nygin will be running with you today. As you know, it's their first day, so show them what to do."

Jal and Nygin were Collie pups, and like all new recruits, they were young, just three months old. When he looked at them, Lido saw himself, Raffle, and Skil at that age, arriving at the mine together on their first day of Kaxian duty. He grinned at the fond memory.

Both of the new recruits' tails were under their bellies, wagging quickly.

Lido stood up straight, raised up his tail, and went over to meet them, letting his tail wag ever so slowly.

Skil followed Lido, also letting her tail wag slowly.

Lido looked both puppies in the eyes, "Hello, I'm Lido, and this is my mate, Skil. Have a seat."

Both puppies dutifully sat as they said together, "Hello, Lido. Hello, Skil."

The puppies had sat on their tails, which kept wagging furiously in front of their bellies.

Lido smiled at them a little, to show that he was friendly, but not too much, or they'd think he was soft. He said, "I know that yesterday at Kaxian Headquarters, Heg explained scouting duty to you."

Both puppies said, "Yes, Lido!"

"Good, I see he explained how you are to address me. He must have also explained how important it is that you obey my every command, immediately."

Jal and Nygin both rolled over and exposed their bellies to Lido, to show him they knew he was boss.

"Very good. Let's see how you do. Scouts, stand up!"

Both puppies jumped up, only wobbling a little.

"Scouts, run up to the mine entrance!"

They all 4 ran up there and stood looking out at the open desert. It stretched on for a few miles and then ended in rocky brown hills. Lido made sure his scouts knew how to tell him where they had spotted a Nique.

That was the point of their scouting duty, after all: to guard the mine from Niques. They didn't want the Niques to steal any of the jex the rest of the pack were mining.

"Scouts, how would you tell me if there were a Nique by that boulder?"

"Nique, 4 o'clock," both puppies said.

"Good, and on that little hill?"

"Nique, 11 o'clock."

Lido looked them both in the eyes again and said, "Scouts, what do you never do?"

"Never chase Niques!" both puppies said together.

Jal rolled his eyes when he said it, but it was the right answer, so Lido figured he had that part of the drill covered.

Lido said, "Good, scouts. Let's go on patrol!"

With that, they all took off at a slow run. Skil started to take her usual place in front, defending the leader.

Lido said, "Skil, run behind me."

She looked at him sideways with her eyebrows perched.

Lido said, "I need to defend us now." He didn't want to mention their unborn pups out loud, but she seemed to catch on.

She wagged her tail and got behind him, followed by Nygin, then Jal. Lido was glad they were behind her, even if they didn't realize they were guarding his mate's back.

The open desert stretched out from 8 o'clock to 4 o'clock, with the human civilization sprawling behind them.

Lido worried less about seeing Niques in the open desert. It was dry, and there were rattlesnakes. Niques were too spoiled to wander out there. That was a good reason to patrol it anyway, though. Niques were also clever and scheming.

Still, from experience, Lido knew that his scouting party was most likely to spot loose Niques inside the human civilization. And that's just where the party did spot loose Niques.

"Niques, 12 o'clock!" everyone said at once.

A few blocks down the street, an older human was sitting on a low wall, playing with her cell phone. In front of her on the watered grass, seven unleashed Niques jumped around, playing some stupid Nique game. They were of a few different Nique breeds: 4 Yorkshire Terriers, 2 Papillons, and 1 Chihuahua. (In Southern California, there's always a Chihuahua.)

Lido barked out a relay message in Kanx, the secret code language of the Kaxians.

"Seven loose Niques, 5 o'clock, perimeter B."

The Niques were at 5 o'clock to the mine, even though they were at noon to the scouting patrol. Perimeter B told the pack how far away the Niques were from the mine.

The other scouting party answered.

"5 o'clock B, aye."

All set to continue their run so that the Niques wouldn't suspect the nearby mining activity, Lido skidded to a stop when Nygin yipped.

"Niques approaching!"

Skil took over relaying messages to the rest of the pack in Kanx so that Lido was free to take charge of their encounter with the Niques.

"Niques approaching, 5 o'clock B!"

Half of the loose Niques, 3 Yorkshire Terriers and the Chihuahua, ran toward Lido's scouting party, tails up and wagging quickly, ears up. They were taunting the new recruits. First the Chihuahua would say something mean, and then the 3 Yorkshire Terriers would copy him and be mean, too.

"Aw! Isn't that sweet?"

"Look, the little puppies are out with their babysitters!"

"Stay close to the grown-ups, pups."

"Yeah, we wouldn't want you to get lost!"

Jal lunged out at the Niques, growling and whining in the little puppy voice most Kaxians only use to make humans do what they want.

Jal said, "Lido! Did you hear that? Let's get them!"

"Jal, stand down. They're trying to get you riled up. Don't let them. You're bigger than that."

19

The Niques crossed the street, probably to go around Lido's party and look for the mine. As Niques are prone to do, they kept on sassing the bigger Kaxians, taking care to focus on the smallest.

"What's the matter, little puppy?"

"Do you miss your mommy?"

"Are you scared to be alone?"

Lido looked over at Skil. She smiled at him and rolled her eyes, showing him she thought the Niques were being stupid, too.

Growling, Jal took off running after the Niques.

Lido felt bad for making fun of the situation just then. He was often on the case of other scout trainers for not realizing the younger Kaxians didn't have enough experience with the Niques' bullying behavior to see how ridiculous they were, picking on dogs three times their size.

Lido put command in his voice.

"Jal, don't chase!"

The Collie pup didn't even turn his head to look at Lido. He kept right on running after the Niques, telling them what for.

"Shut up, you little toy dogs! I'm bigger than you, and when I catch you, you'll wish you had kept your mouths shut!"

Aside from getting angry at Jal now for ignoring and disobeying him, Lido had two problems with Jal chasing the four Niques:

One: that little Chihuahua was running extra fast! Even at three months old, Jal was much bigger and should have caught it already. Something odd was up with the Nique's speed.

Two: no one could be sure where the Niques would run to. Yes, they were probably looking for the

Kaxians' mine. But there was a chance they would lead Jal into a trap. For this reason, the Kaxians' rule for new scouts was "Don't chase."

However, it's easy to tell a pup not to chase; it's difficult for a pup to actually not chase.

Lido tried one last time to command Jal to quit chasing.

"Jal! Come back here now!"

It was a lost cause. Jal appeared so intent on catching his prey that he was oblivious to Lido's voice.

Jal and the super-fast Nique were several blocks down the street now. They might turn at any moment and be more difficult to follow.

It hurt Lido's pride to admit to himself that he'd lost control of the situation, but it would hurt things a whole lot worse if anything happened to Jal.

"Scouts! After Jal!"

Lido and Nygin took off after Jal right away.

"Jal's chasing and we're in pursuit," Lido heard Skil tell the pack in Kanx, and then he was relieved to hear her running behind him. He slowed just a bit, to let his mate catch up.

He heard the Niques barking in a language he didn't understand, and he heard responses coming back in that same language. That couldn't be good.

Chapter 3: Baj

Baj the Chihuahua puppy ran into the orange kitchen, turned around, and ran full speed on the flat brown carpet toward the high yellow wrap-around couch, where all the humans sat with yummy food smells—chicken enchiladas!

He raced past Mom, Dad, two high-top sneakers that were taller than him, his four brothers, and his three sisters. He bounded half-way up the front of the couch and scrambled his paws, trying to stay up there where the food was. He smelled it and could almost taste it. His mouth watered.

And, he fell down on his butt.

Bonk!

His sisters—Pim, Cor, and Sah—all laughed at Baj, wagging their tails and jumping around, they enjoyed his failure so much.

Pim said, "Ha ha! You fell!" She stuck her tongue out at Baj.

Cor and Sah joined in, sticking their tongues out, too, copycats that they were. "Ha ha!"

Gat rolled his eyes at Baj from his position under the coffee table. Baj didn't understand Gat. He never wanted to play. He was always studying the humans' gadgets. Right now, he was watching the humans' hands as they controlled their joysticks, and then

23

turning around to see what was happening on the TV. How boring!

Before Baj could get up, Mof's foot hit the top of his head. His one bigger brother had run up and used him for a stepping stone to the couch.

Baj laughed when Mof still didn't make it up to the food, even though Mof fell on top of him.

"Oof!" Baj said.

Tef the copycat brother ran, climbed up both Baj and Mof—and made it up onto the couch! One of the humans picked Tef up and was petting him. He tried to explain to the humans they were supposed to give him food.

"I made it up here! Give me some of those enchiladas! Hey! Be fair!"

But the humans couldn't understand what Tef was saying, of course.

Baj figured maybe if he hurried and got up there while the human was still petting Tef, then Baj would get some of the food. But he wasn't the only puppy thinking that way.

Baj saw Elp come running. Before another foot hit his head, Baj got right back up, ran into the kitchen again, and stopped. His ears went back, and he slammed his front paws down on the orange linoleum floor.

"Move, Sah!"

"I am moving," Sah said, wriggling around like she was having trouble getting up.

"Move faster, or I'll run you over!"

Sah took a deep breath, raised her head up, and at the top of her voice yelled out, "Mom! Baj is bossing me around again!"

That's when the biggest human almost tripped

over Sah on his way back to the couch from the refrigerator with his bottle of soda.

Sah was OK.

But the fun was over for now.

The big human told one of the little humans to put Baj and his family outside.

The little human was nice about it, but he did insist that everyone go out.

The sun was setting over the wooden fence that surrounded their sparsely grassed and mostly dry world. The fence shadows looked extra dark beside the sandy desert soil that reflected the sunlight with glints of copper and zinc.

Even though the houses were far apart with big yards in between, the scents of all the neighbors cooking dinner reached Baj's nose from up to a mile away. Yum! His stomach growled, but he knew he'd be fed soon, so he didn't worry about it, not too much.

Once they were all outside, Baj's parents went to yell at the big cream-colored Kaxian mom in the yard northwest of them, across the dirt alley in back of their humans' den.

Her humans called her Buttons, and she was always out there, tied to the back fence, surrounded by her four puppies. They weren't tied up.

Mom started. "Buttons, are you nursing those puppies enough?"

Dad joined in. "They look really skinny to me."

"They aren't warm enough," Mom said.

"Maybe you should eat more so you can keep them warmer," Dad said.

"Oh yeah, your humans don't feed you enough," Mom said.

This was normal. It went on every day, especially when Buttons's humans were outside with her. Buttons growled at Mom and Dad, but they were talking through two fences and a dirt alley, so she couldn't do anything to them. Soon, Buttons's humans started yelling, too. These humans spoke English, while Baj's parents' humans spoke Spanish, but Baj and his family understood them all.

"Buttons, quit bothering those dogs next door!"

"Shut your trap!"

"They'll shut up if you shut up!"

"They're itty bitty little things."

"Leave them alone!"

Buttons whimpered at that, and rolled over onto her back to expose her belly and tell her humans she knew they were boss.

Baj figured Buttons must be a really bad mom, because Mom and Dad were constantly having to tell her how she should be doing things.

The weirdest thing was, Mom and Dad never talked with Buttons about how it was the Kaxians against the Niques. Buttons was a Kaxian, and Baj and his family were Niques, so really, Baj wondered why his parents tried so hard to help her. Why did they care so much?

What's more, Mom and Dad had told Baj and his brothers and sisters not to bring up the struggle between Kaxians and Niques, either. They were never to call Buttons a Kaxian or even mention Kaxians or Niques around her. And she never called them Niques. They were forbidden to talk to her or any of the other Kaxians around them about it at all.

It was all very confusing.

Oh well.

Every kid knows that grown-ups give you weird orders that they won't explain.

"Don't mention Niques or Kaxians to the Kaxians next door" was just something Baj's parents always said. It sounded no weirder to him than "Don't talk with your mouth full," so the Nique puppies didn't think anything of it.

They just obeyed it.

Glad that a dirt alley ran between the yards and prevented the Kaxian pups from digging their way to them, the Nique pups reported in to their senior Nique for duty. To the humans inside the house, it just sounded like the puppies were barking for no reason.

"Mof reporting in for duty!"

"Baj reporting in for duty!"

"Tef reporting in for duty!"

"Gat reporting in for duty!"

"Pim reporting in for duty!"

"Cor reporting in for duty!"

"Elp reporting in for duty!"

"Sah reporting in for duty!"

Sounding to the humans like barking from far away, the puppies' senior Nique gave the usual directions.

"Continue digging the tunnel."

Baj ran to be the first one through the hole they had dug under the wooden fence on the west side of their yard, but Mof beat him to it by half a second. Nosing into the space next to his brother, Baj tried to push Mof out of the way and be the first one through. Mof's left front paw landed squarely on Baj's right eye.

"Ouch! Hey, no reason to blind me!"

"Yeah, yeah. Just wait your turn. I'm the first one through!"

"Well, I'm the second one through!"

"Third!" Tef called out as he wriggled under the fence.

Several pushings, pawings, and scufflings later, all eight of the puppies were on the other side of the wooden fence and racing to their tunnel, which started on the far side of the yard next door.

Mof had a head start, so he remained in the lead.

Elp and Sah were the runts, and they lagged behind.

As they ran, Baj and his siblings all sniffed the air near the empty human den next door, making sure no humans had moved in.

So far, so good.

Different groups of humans came and looked at the human den every few days, and had been doing so ever since Baj could remember, but no specific human scent persisted.

The puppies also smelled the gophers who lived underground here, and the cat hair that lingered in the trees. They smelled the Rottweiler Kaxians who lived over their tunnel. There was also the scent of horses in the western yard, but that was an old, old scent, at least as old as Mom and Dad. Ancient.

Yesterday, a group of young humans had been inside the small shed out behind the human den for hours. They'd been laughing, talking, and keeping the Niques from digging their tunnel. It had been almost worth the delay when the puppies found food wrappers in the shed that made good licking. They tasted like hamburgers and tacos.

The day before yesterday, a hawk had swooped

down from one of the tall pine trees and almost scooped up Elp. Dad had used his super Nique speed to run at the hawk and scare it away. Baj had been surprised. He knew Dad shouldn't have used super Nique speed so close to the humans. Not in broad daylight. Dad must really love Elp.

Almost every day, something tried to eat the Nique puppies. Snakes and gophers popped out of holes and tried to grab them. Hawks and crows came out of the sky or the trees without much warning at all. Kaxians dug into this yard or their yard and attacked (which was odd, because Mom and Dad made sure that the Kaxians around here didn't know they were Kaxians).

On the other days, humans came looking at the human den, making the Chihuahua puppies wait hours before they dared to go near their tunnel.

The small Niques were aware of the danger from the gophers, the humans, the cats, the birds of prey, and the four large Kaxians who lived over or near their tunnel site: two Rottweilers, a Pit Bull, and a Bull Mastiff. But Nique Duty made the puppies go dig the tunnel.

One thing was in their favor: it was winter. So long as it wasn't raining or snowing, winter was a good time of year for Niques to be out digging tunnels here in the high desert. The grass was tall enough to hide a grown Chihuahua, let alone puppies. This was a desert. The ground only froze once every twenty years or so. It didn't rain or snow often, but it did happen. It only rained enough to make grass grow in winter.

So they had to cross the large backyard next door to get to their tunnel. Running was the best way to avoid danger.

Mof and Baj were in the lead, followed a little ways

behind by Tef and Gat.

And then Pim and Cor.

Then a long break.

Elp and Sah were in their usual place, far at the back.

All of them could see the welcoming brown of the tunnel up ahead, going under the western chain link fence, just big enough for a grown Chihuahua or two puppies.

Just keep running, each puppy told him or herself.

Keep running and you'll make it. No problem.

Baj heard the cat in the tree a second before he heard it drop through the branches.

"CAT!" Baj yelled as he whirled around to see.

The cat was huge, tabby striped, and dropping right down onto Pim!

Pim was just standing there with her mouth wide open, watching the cat fall down closer and closer to her.

Baj yelled some more. "You leave my sister alone, you big ugly cat!"

Cor shoved Pim out of the way at the last second.

Dad was there now, yelling at the cat, too. "You leave our babies alone!"

Baj was confused. Where had Dad just come from? He hadn't been there a second ago.

Whoa, Mom was here by his side now, too! She was growling at the cat. Huh?

Baj looked back and forth at his parents, and then way over to the hole under the eastern fence where they had to have come from. There was no way they could get here so fast! Yet, here they were.

The next thing Baj knew, Mom was biting down hard on one of the cat's hind legs, and Dad on the other.

"MerOWwwwwwwwwwwwL!"

The cat dragged her legs back, spun about looking at all the angry Nique faces, turned, and ran up and over the chain link fence into the back alley.

All the puppies ran to Mom and Dad, nuzzling and kissing them.

"How did you get here so fast, Momma?" Sah said.

"You were all the way over in our yard yelling at Buttons!" Tef said.

"I love you, Mom and Dad!" Pim said, squishing in between them and licking both their faces.

Mom and Dad looked at each other. Dad shook his head no. They kissed and hugged all their children by turn, oldest to youngest, and then Mom urged them all to their duty.

"Run to your tunnel, kids!"

"We've got your backs!"

The puppies took off toward the beckoning brown mouth of their tunnel.

Chapter 4: Neya

Nanny Fon had died defending the new wolf puppies from a recent attack by coyotes. The scout, Porl, had notified the pack in time for them to kill most of the coyotes, but Nanny Fon was gone.

The pack's alpha male, Scur, had promoted Belg up to the scout position and promoted Porl to join the hunters, as a reward for bringing the pack in time to save the puppies. Porl was one of Neya's litter mates. He walked much taller now that he ran with the hunters.

Neya noticed that Belg watched sadly whenever his own litter mates ran off with the hunters. She also saw that Ordn, Tolt, and Kess never noticed their littermate Belg's sad face. They were too busy being glad they ran with the hunters now.

The pack's alpha female, Fleek, had made Neya her new official nanny wolf.

Neya was a responsible grown-up now at two years old, which was older than half the wolves in the pack. She had a new litter of brothers and sisters to babysit while almost everyone's mother, Fleek the alpha female, was off hunting with the pack.

Patiently, Neya cleaned the wax from Stulp's ear. The female pup stretched out her front paws as far as they would go and yawned a big long yawn, wagging her tail.

Stulp's yawn was contagious, and Neya yawned, too. She envied Stulp her absolute contentment. Neya had been content once with her role in the pack. Now, she wanted more. She wanted pups of her own to raise. She had seen them in a dream, once, more than a year ago.

Oh, she was proud of what she'd already accomplished. The last litter of pups she'd raised had turned out very well, three good hunters and a good scout.

Glar's wobbly legs were trying to carry him outside the cave.

Neya rose to her full height, planted her front paws quickly, and called him to him.

"Glar! Come back."

"But I need to..."

"I'll clean it up. You must stay inside the cave. It's for your own safety."

"Aw, can't we go outside? We've been inside all day!"

"No. Not until the pack gets back."

Glar's ears and tail went down, and his shoulders slumped.

Neya tried to explain why the pack being gone was a good thing.

"They'll bring more meat when they come home!"

Glar's tail started wagging.

Neya smiled. "Yep! That's why they have to go, so they can bring meat."

"I guess that's OK, then." Glar perked up and trotted back to his nanny.

She nuzzled him and licked the goop out of his eyes.

Caring for this new batch of brothers and sisters on her own while the pack hunted was exhausting. With the pack gone and no one to help escort the pups outside, clean up after them, feed them, and keep them quiet, Nanny Neya's only break was while all the puppies slept.

If she were the Alpha female of her own pack, then she could be the one out hunting, and one of her own grown daughters would be staying home as the nanny. Yes, that was what she wanted. Now if only a male lone wolf would come calling for her...

Still daydreaming, Neya chewed up some of the meat the pack had left and passed some into each pup's waiting mouth. The pups had been weaned yesterday and couldn't quite eat on their own yet. They were always hungry.

The pups were always thirsty, too.

"Filp! Crom! Stulp! Glar!"

"Yes, Neya!"

"Remember, stay inside! I'll be back with water for you first, Filp."

All the puppies rolled over onto their backs to let Neya know she was boss.

Filp smiled at her before he rolled over.

Some boss she was! Yeah, puppies rolled over for her while they were young and helpless and she still fed them, but as soon as they could eat on their own, they would be independent of her and given their own assignments. She hadn't been completely in charge of the last litter because Fon had still been alive, but she knew what was coming soon.

Neya thought fondly of the puppies in the first litter she'd cared for. Ordn, Tolt, and Kess had been allowed out hunting with the pack for almost a year

35

now. Belg stayed home with her, but as a scout. At first, Porl had stayed too and trained him, but now Belg was a full defender scout on his own. Being a scout looked like a lot more fun than being a nanny. All Belg did was run around all day and have fun chasing squirrels!

Sniffing the air outside first to make sure no predators lurked, Neya went out to the nearby trickle of water down from the snowy peak, which had made the pack choose this small cave. It filled up a small puddle where Neya drank her fill and then made eight trips back and forth, two mouthfuls of water for each pup. She gave them the water the same way she gave them the meat, passing it straight from her mouth to theirs.

She wished sometimes that she never had seen that vision of how life could be so different for her, if she were the alpha female of her own pack. She wanted to be content. The vision had ruined her contentment, yet she had to do her duty anyway. It wasn't fair.

When Neya returned to the cave for the eighth time that hour, Filp had found a cricket in one of the cracks in the cave wall. His tail wagged gleefully behind him while his little paws jabbed toward the cricket. They were still too clumsy to quite reach in and kill it, but he sure was trying.

Neya watched Filp with admiration. OK, and she harbored a little envy. Some amusement crept in when he barked at the cricket.

Filp's little tail was out wagging as he romped from one crack to the next, following the cricket as it jumped around. Each time he romped, he called out to the cricket.

"Come out, Cricket!"

"Get out here and let me kill you!"

"I see you in there!"

"You can't hide!"

An hour after the last feeding, Neya fed all the pups again, made them promise to stay inside again, and again went to sniff outside and make sure no predators lurked between the cave and the small trickle of water that ensured her family's survival, or anywhere nearby.

This time, she smelled trouble.

"Belg! Come quick!"

In the distance, Neya heard Belg's reply.

"On my way! What is it?"

"Too many deer! They'll drink all our water! There must be ten of them!"

Belg said something she hoped the puppies didn't repeat when their parents were home.

Deer didn't usually come this far south. They liked it better up north where there was more greenery to eat. Neya and her pack would be going up there themselves, come spring. The extra rain down here this year must have made the deer venture farther south than usual, out of the cold.

Neya felt her heart beating faster. It urged her to go out and shoo the deer away from the pack's water. The puppies would go thirsty if all those deer drank from their little pond.

But she had to stay with the pups in case a predator came. Nature is cruel, and Neya's instincts told her the chances of a predator coming while she and Belg had the deer and the water to worry about were good.

Finally, she saw Belg run by. She barely heard him speak.

"I hear the deer. I'll try to turn them away from our water."

A few seconds went by, and then she heard Belg shooing the deer.

"Get away! This is our water! There's more in the next canyon! Go over there!"

She wasn't at all sure the deer understood what Belg was saying, but his voice echoed off the canyons. If she didn't know better, she would think ten more wolves were coming down to join him. She stood tall in the cave mouth.

Pride surged within her as she watched Belg herd the deer. No, she hadn't taught him to know which one of this herd was the lead deer or to run up to the lead deer and bite at its legs so that it turned, not directly.

However, she had been the one to tell Belg the story of the deer. The tale showed all young wolves how deer should be handled, in a general way. Neya knew that Belg's effectiveness was largely to her credit. That gave her some job satisfaction.

She watched him skillfully run in, nip at the key deer's legs, then run out, turning the herd. While he was out, he barked up into the canyon in strategic places so that his barks echoed back to the deer and made them think more wolves were coming.

For Neya, watching Belg turn the deer was entertainment, like watching people dance is for humans. Turning deer was a wolf art form.

There was music to go along with the deer dance, too. The deer's hooves made a thunderous sound as they raced by the cave. The sound modulated whenever the herd turned, and it got louder when it entered the cave and bounced around inside, looking for a way out. There was an eerie rhythm to it that she found pleasing.

She stood in the mouth of the cave and watched Belg long enough to be sure the deer kept right on running and didn't deplete the pack's water. She smiled at Belg once the deer were gone, and he raised his nose to her as he left to run his scouting patrol around the cave again.

"Tell us a story, Neya."

This was Crom talking now, the runt of this new litter.

Neya sighed. Part of her duty as nanny was to tell the puppies stories—both to teach them wolf ways and to keep them from missing their mother. The trouble was, the story of warning against the dog aliens was the next one up for her to tell. It was about how the dog aliens had come to their world from another world out there in the stars thousands of years ago. The story showed that the dog aliens were the wolves' enemies, and it told how bad an idea trusting the dog aliens was.

Because of a vision Neya had seen of herself starting a family with one dog alien in particular, she found telling that story difficult. She didn't want to tell it. She knew she would have to eventually, but she just couldn't bear it right now, for some odd reason.

Neya smiled at Crom and started a different story, one that suited their situation. Surely, that was appropriate.

"Do you know who Woll the Scout was?"

All the puppies spoke at once, jumping up and wiggling their tails as fast as they would go.

"Yes!"

"Tell me, Stulp."

"Woll the Scout protected the puppies while his pack was out hunting!"

All the puppies were still jumping around and wagging their little tails.

"That's right! How did he protect them, Glar?"

"He ran and he ran around their den!"

"Yes! What did he do while he ran, Crom?"

"He sniffed the air!"

"Yes! What was he trying to scent, Filp?"

"Meanies who would try to eat the puppies!"

"That's right!"

All the puppies were fully engaged in helping Neya tell the story. Their tails were out and wagging. Their ears were up and alert. Their tongues hung out of their mouths, which were all smiling. They skipped around and around her, excited. From memories of being a puppy herself, Neya knew that each pup played the role of Woll the scout in his or her imagination.

"What did Woll do if a meanie came to try and get the puppies, Crom?"

"He howled to the alpha male!"

"That's right! And then what did Woll do, Glar?"

"He ran to the puppies and stood in the way!"

"Yes! Show me how you run to the puppies here and stand in the way so nothing can come in the cave and eat them!"

All the puppies bravely stood in the cave mouth, fending off the imaginary meanies from coming to eat the imaginary littler puppies.

Neya felt a little guilty for thinking earlier that Belg was just running around. She knew better. He was doing the essential task of making sure she and the puppies ate and drank in peace. He had come right away when she called, too, without any of the sass that Porl used to give their old nanny, Fon.

Yes, she had a right to feel proud of the job she'd done teaching Belg and his litter mates. He was a fine scout, and Ordn, Tolt, and Kess were fine hunters. Soon, they would be back with more meat.

Chapter 5: Raffle

I'll wager my humans had second thoughts about Oreo almost right away—and third, fourth, fifth, even sixth thoughts. I pride myself on being a 'good boy'. I try my hardest to figure out what my humans want, and then I do my best to do what they want me to.

Up until Oreo joined our pack, I could count on one paw the number of times my humans had said, "No!"

Now, they were saying, "No!" every time I turned around! I started to get paranoid. I was pretty sure they were talking to Oreo whenever they said, "No!" He was a bad boy who seemed to get a thrill out of making them say, "No!" However, unless they said, "Oreo! No!" I could never be positive they weren't yelling at me. This was nerve-wracking.

There I would be, minding my own business, lounging on my living room bed and cleaning Oreo's earwax off my nails. And then I'd hear it.

"No!"

Guilt would seize me. Full of guilt at having displeased my humans, I would jump up off my bed. I'd be thinking, "OK! I thought that was my bed, but if you say so, then I'll stay off of it. But you don't have to yell. Just tell me once. I'm a good boy. I'll listen."

Or I'd be giving my no-longer-stuffed dragon a bath, practicing because my mistress had given me the job of pack nanny: first for Oreo, whom she thought was a puppy, and I was sure later I'd be the nanny for her own young.

"No!"

Feeling horrible, I would jump up and leave the little no-longer-stuffed dragon alone.

And I would think, "OK! I thought that was my toy, but if you say so, then I won't give it a bath. But please don't yell at me. Don't you know I'm a good boy?"

I'd be shaking, I was so guilt-ridden at having displeased my master or mistress.

Every time, it would turn out my humans were yelling at Oreo, not me.

He was constantly getting into things or trying to pee on the floor. Oreo always had a scowl on his face when the humans weren't looking, even when he was lying on the comfy bed they had bought for him. He scratched at the carpet like it was leaves outside.

You would think Oreo had never been in a human's den before.

That was silly, though.

Wasn't it?

Could a Kaxian get to be three years old without going into a human's den?

No, that wasn't possible in this day and age.

Later that evening, our humans were both reading books in the pack's sleeping den while Oreo and I got acquainted in the living room. It had a shoe rack by the front door, a huge stone fireplace, a TV and stereo, and a black leather couch.

The humans weren't around, so I had to be the

one to yell at Oreo.

"Oreo! Stay off the couch! No! Don't chew shoes!"

Of course, the rascal wouldn't listen to me.

"Will you relax?" Oreo said. "You're more uptight than the humans."

"They don't know what you're doing in here!"

"Yeah, and what they don't know won't hurt them, Uptight Dog."

"She will be upset if you chew up her shoes!"

"She won't spank me."

"Put that shoe down right now!"

"Make me."

I was going to have to make him, but I couldn't let him guess how I did it. I shook my head at him and went down the hall, to make him think I had given up in disgust.

I could hear Oreo, still chewing on our mistress's shoe, growling and grunting as if he were killing it.

OK, time to make him stop. In my mind's eye, I composed a little movie for Oreo. In it, he put the shoe back in the shoe bin and then lay down on the orange shag carpet, chewing on what was left of my favorite toy, the empty skin of the stuffed dragon my master had given back when I was still teething.

Popping sounds came from the living room, where Oreo had probably broken part of that shoe.

Closing my eyes, I concentrated on Oreo's mind. There it was: slightly red with anger but still accessible, if I concentrated. I uploaded my mental movie and played it for him, watching his mind's aura change from red anger to yellow scheming.

I chuckled to myself. Let him scheme against my toys rather than our mistress's shoes! I was a year-old adult and over my attachment to my toys. I only played with them now to show appreciation to my humans for supplying them. I always ended up giving them baths instead of chewing on them.

Our mistress was training me to care for the young in our pack. She started with Oreo, and that was unfortunate, but I would make her happy and do as she said, of course. Besides, it would be great when she finally had babies for me to care for! I was excited about my future as our pack's nanny.

Of course, Oreo was taking advantage of the situation.

"Hey, Uptight Dog! Come clean my ears; they're getting really waxy."

Oreo sidled up to where our mistress was petting me, presenting me his ears to clean.

I licked the wax out of his ears.

Come on! I had to.

She was watching, and anyway, I was bonded to her. She had told me to take care of him, and I had to obey her commands.

Oreo was a jerk about it, though.

"Don't worry: there'll be dirtier areas for you to clean later, after she lets us out."

I know it was immature of me, but you know my frustration at having to care for a 'baby brother' who was really two years older than me?

I took it out on the cat.

For deliberately peeing on my sleeping bag, she had been relegated to spending the rest of her days shut into our huge bathroom. Our humans went in there often, and I followed them in whenever I could. Since our mistress was training me to care for her future young and making me practice on Oreo, I figured I should practice on the cat, too. Oh, how she growled and fussed whenever I gave her a bath!

"MMMMmmmrrrrrrOOOooowwllll!"

Our mistress loved my attention to my 'cat sister' and encouraged me.

"Aw, Puritan. Mommy Raffle's just giving you a nice bath. It's OK."

I'm bonded to our humans, so I don't mind our mistress calling me Mommy Raffle. I know that's sissy. Part of being a grown-up is accepting that you are going to do some sissy things and even enjoy them. Our mistress had given me the role of nanny in the pack. That's an important job. I accepted this duty with love and keen anticipation of the time I would be caring for her pups.

I did my best to keep Oreo in line with my mental movies, but I had to sleep sometime, and he knew it. Well, he knew I couldn't tell on him while I was sleeping, not that I could somewhat control him while I was awake. That is, if he wasn't too emotional, I could.

Oreo dug out of our yard that very first night.

I had fallen asleep on the living room floor, lulled by the sounds of the cop show our master was watching. Our mistress let Oreo out into the back yard to do his business, and in the cover of darkness he dug his way out under the fence. I found out about it pretty quick when I was woken up by my mistress's yelling.

"Scott! Oreo's not in the yard!"

"Did we leave the gate open?"

"No!"

I searched for Oreo's mind, but he was already out of my mental range. I had no clue where he was.

There were many Kaxian minds nearby, though, so I was sure Kax would help me find him. I kept trying.

We all tramped through the sliding glass door into our back yard. It was a grassy square about 50 feet on each side. My master shined his flashlight around the bottom of the wooden fence. Out loud, I told every Kaxian within earshot what was going on, making it sound to my humans like I was howling in sympathy to their distress:

"My humans adopted another Kaxian today, and I've just found his dig-out. He's not anyone I know. He's part English Springer Spaniel and part Border Collie this life. Sorry, I don't even know his Kaxian name yet. He's mostly black with white splotches and speckles, about three years old, and really obnoxious. Please, if you recognize his description, let me know right away what his Kaxian name and duty are, and warn his pack that my master is looking for him."

My humans found the hole a minute after I had.

"Oh no. See here where he dug under the fence?"

"Uh! What do we do?"

I knew that the only chance my humans had of getting Oreo home again was if they took me out looking for him and I managed to get close enough to play Oreo a mental movie of him coming home with us. I wished I could just let Oreo run away and be rid of him, but my mistress had ordered me to keep him from running away. I didn't think she knew I understood her command, but that didn't make it any less compulsive. I was going to do everything in my power to get the big stinker back—and then I was going to be very angry with him.

Right then, all I could think about was the best way to get Oreo back.

We would have to go in our little Nissan truck because there was no way my master could run fast enough to catch up with Oreo. He was probably miles away by now.

I played my master a mental movie of the two of us driving off in the truck and my mistress staying home and letting Oreo in when he came home on his own.

It worked.

"You stay here in case he comes home. Raffle and I will go look for Oreo. Come on, Boy!"

I barked to my pack then, using the timing to make it seem like I was responding to my master's enthusiasm.

"My human is taking me out in the truck to look for our new Kaxian, whom they call Oreo. Let me know if you see him."

Of course, our pesky Nique neighbors got their humans to let them outside so they could nose into our business. They knew just what to say to hurt my feelings.

"Ha ha!"

"Raffle lost his 'baby brother' already!"

"Some pack nanny you are!"

"Can't even care for one puppy!"

Glad to have something I was allowed to take my anger out on, I played mental movies for the squirrels in the nearby trees, showing them throwing pine cones at my pesky Nique neighbors. Squirrels are good at throwing things!

Bop!

Wham!

I got some cheap satisfaction out of hearing Cherry and Fred cry out in pain.

"Ouch!"

"Hey!"

"Watch it!"

My master and I got in our truck. He put my harness on and buckled me into the passenger seat for safety, the way he did when we guarded construction sites together at night. He started up the truck and drove out of our cul-de-sac.

The lack of any report on the Kaxian duty my new 'baby brother' performed disturbed me more than his running away. In addition to the 'bark relay', I was using mental channels to ask for any information anyone had on him. The lack of any response surprised me and made me uneasy.

When I finally realized my mistake, apologized, and asked Kax directly in my mind for the answers, I was shocked at the messages I received from the various Kaxian minds close by me:

"Oreo's Kaxian name is Ferd."

"Raffle, be careful. Ferd doesn't know he's a Kaxian."

"He was born and raised in ignorance, so his Kaxian memories have not awakened."

"Ferd represses the memories."

"This life, Ferd has only served the humans, never done any Kaxian duty."

"No humans can know that dogs are aliens."

Well, that last part didn't surprise me. That had been drilled into me ever since I could remember, by every Kaxian I had ever met and by Kax directly in my mind, too. But what came next was almost more than I could take.

"Your Kaxian duty is to bring Ferd back to us."

"Make 'Oreo' understand that he's a Kaxian."

Chapter 6: Oreo

Oreo here. Yeah, I was not going to stay in that joint one minute past when Uptight Dog fell asleep. I was a free spirit; you couldn't put chains on me. Well, not for long, anyway.

Not only had they put a harness on me and seat-belted me in the truck, they were going to make me sleep in a cage! Just like the one my last human had abandoned me in.

No thanks. No way. No how.

That male human had paid good money for me, so he would come looking. I knew I'd best go where his truck couldn't get to me. That meant the rugged hills that surrounded this unnaturally green suburban desert community. There were many dog trails there, and I always picked the turn going up.

I thought by getting out of town I would escape the scents of my fellow dogs and not just the humans, but I was wrong. These trails were covered in dog paw prints, and dog scent permeated the area.

It was weird.

I was pretty far from home, though. I'd been raised on a farm up on the I-5 grapevine. Back home, in sparsely populated farm country, I had never run away because everyone within a hundred miles knew who I was and where I was supposed to be.

Maybe my suburban brethren got out more. Heh! Yeah, that must be it. Getting out was easier here in the suburbs, just a matter of digging under a fence. Why was I surprised that I wasn't the only one who thought of digging out?

I got up near the top of the group of hills, and wouldn't you know it, someone had parked some kind of RV up there. It baffled me how they got it up there on these narrow trails, but the fact remained it was there. The real kicker was it didn't smell like humans, just dogs.

A German Shepherd and a Great Dane were sitting outside the RV, guarding it from what I could tell. They must have been there an awfully long time, because their humans were long gone, leaving no trace of scent.

Weird.

They didn't seem starved, and they weren't tied up. They spoke to me in this weird slang I couldn't understand. I'd heard a lot of barking all the time since I'd come out here to the suburbs, but I couldn't quite understand. It sounded like I should be able to make sense of it, but I couldn't. These two seemed really excited about something. They planted their paws in front of them and quickly lowered their heads while they spoke, sure signs of being serious. They obviously wanted me to help them.

I didn't trust the dogs around here. Not yet, anyway. They weren't like the country dogs I was used to. No, these suburban dogs wandered around and talked funny.

Since they were using slang, maybe these suburban dogs were up to something. I didn't want to take part in anything I didn't understand, so I kept going on up into the hills, hoping if I went far enough I would escape the scent of fellow dogs in addition to losing the scent of humans.

I felt some relief when those two didn't follow me, but I shuddered at all the slang they barked out and when others barked back to them.

I felt like an idiot up here in the wild hills wearing the new blue collar those humans had put on me, so as soon as I felt safe from being followed I hooked that collar on the bare branch of a low bush and pulled it off. There. That was more like it. Just me and my considerable amount of fur.

Full of dog food, I didn't need to hunt for my dinner, but I knew how, so I wasn't worried about where my meals would come from out here in the wild. Most dogs don't know how to hunt. Did you know that? Only us hunting dogs have the instinct for it. Other dogs can learn, but they have to be taught by one who knows how to hunt. I smelled all kinds of game up here in these rocky sage-brushy hills that looked bare from below: blue jays, pigeons, squirrels, snakes, rats, mice, raccoons...

This brought back memories of hunting with my buddies back home on the farm, during the happy time before the cage, when they called me Ferd.

Most of the time, we hunted the gophers that threatened our humans' strawberry crops. There were hundreds of gophers every spring, but by fall the pack always had them down to dozens. Hunting in a pack is easy and fun.

"Ferd! You go north side!"

"OK! I'm going north!"

I ran as fast as my legs would take me, over the strawberry rows. It was a race to get the gophers boxed in before they got back to the warren just outside our farm to the north. These pesky gophers ate the strawberries we were guarding. Guarding the humans' strawberries was our job, the reason our humans gave us water in the summer and warm dry places to sleep in the winter. We had to hunt for our food, and the gophers were pretty tasty.

Are you uneasy at my talk of hunting?

Hey, we dogs are organic pest control. Still, we do have to pee now and then. I'm just saying you should wash your strawberries before you eat them, even organic strawberries.

I could see the gophers running for their warren, a dozen of them or more. We had them on the run, alright. My job was to get in front of them and make them pause long enough that my pack mates could catch them. I was good at my job. I jumped over the strawberry rows, wagging my tail and barking out with the joy of the chase.

I was there! I beat the gophers to the fence. They had dug under the fence, and so had we, but getting under it took too long. Besides, it was a point of honor among us hunters, to catch our prey on our side of the fence. It was a stupid fence: just a few sticks criss crossed here and there. It might keep a cow off our land, but it neither kept us dogs in nor the gophers out.

Planting my front paws, I quickly lowered my head and barked, wagging my tail high in the air because I couldn't contain my energy; I was so pleased with myself.

"Come right to me, you pesky little gophers!"

It worked. The gophers close to me stopped in their tracks. The pack caught up with them from behind, and those gophers were no more.

It was another point of honor among us hunters that no other animals were welcome inside our territory. We knew the humans expected this of us, and we were hungry, so we hunted down every last animal that came inside our fence. Why the humans had put up such a useless fence was beyond us, but we were there to do a job, so we did it. And like I said, hunting in a pack is easy and fun.

I can handle the small pests and prey on my own.

Are you scared of snakes?

Not me. I've killed more than my share of snakes. All I have to do is wait for them to pop out of their hidey holes and bite their heads off. I don't suggest you humans try that, though. Your mouths aren't big enough, for one thing. You're not quick enough, for another.

You humans need us dogs. Just face it.

Birds love to peck at strawberries, and I have stopped my share of birds, too. You don't believe I could catch a bird because they fly, eh? Heh! You must be one of those city or suburban humans. Everyone out on the farms knows about bird dogs, and we Springer Spaniels are bird dogs. I tell you what: birds are complacent in their ability to fly. All I have to do is sneak up behind birds while they are busy pecking into things that don't belong to them. You've never seen a dog sneak? We sneak just like cats do: with our bodies close to the ground, bending our elbows and knees. I can be just as silent as any old cat.

My favorite is catching ducks on the water. Our humans had a swimming pool on their farm, and the ducks thought they were allowed in it. Wrong. They were trespassing! I was the best one at catching things in the water. My fur is so thick that my skin doesn't even get wet unless I'm in the water a long time. I do a great belly flop into a pool, too, if I do say so myself. I swim really well, too. Just as well as any old duck—better, in a fight!

Sometimes, we hunted bigger prey, and that required the pack to work together.

Once a week or so, we chased humans away from the strawberries. Not all of them were strangers, either. You humans are far less respectful of each other's territories than we dogs are.

That rickety old fence kept stray cows off our land. We didn't get anything as big as a cow poking its ugly unwanted face around, but we did get raccoons.

I know. I know.

You're thinking, "What the heck were raccoons doing in the desert?" You think I'm lying. But let me explain a little better where I'm from. Along Interstate 5, California is a watered desert garden. Farmers grow strawberries, grapes, pistachios, peaches, oranges, and all kinds of flowers that they cut and send off in boxes.

Because most of the level land is desert, they have to water it. Have you seen them watering the desert? That's something fun to watch! It's even more fun to watch the humans playing in the water that sprays out from those huge rolling pipes of sprinklers when it's a hundred and ten degrees out in the summer. Even the grown-up humans play in the sprinklers then.

Watering the desert makes more than just farm plants grow. Animals come down from the mountains all around in order to eat all the delicious farm plants. And now we're back to why the humans had me and my pack mates on the strawberry farm.

Raccoons are mean, smart, and strong. That's a bad combination.

One time, this raccoon had worked its way under our humans' den. You know how you humans build your dens up above the ground? Well, our humans' den was so far up off the ground that it had a wooden bottom that rested on top of a ring of stones that was about as tall as me. Here and there, the ring of stones had openings where water pipes and gas pipes came out. These openings were ridiculously big, large enough for a raccoon to get in.

I could understand why it wanted in there. The humans' whole den smelled like food.

Did I tell you that hunting in a pack is easy and fun? It totally is. All we had to do was make sure a few of us were guarding each exit and then send in our three terrier pack members, who were small enough to get in through those holes in the ring of stones.

You should've heard the raccoon shrieking and my terrier pack mates giving him what-for!

Not many humans know this, but terriers are bred for hunting small prey. A terrier's small size allows him to follow gophers and snakes and stuff right down into their burrows. Against three of them, that raccoon didn't stand a chance. He came flying out the hole that I was guarding, the hole in the ring of stones. I had a Coon Hound with me, and I didn't even get a bite in, that Coon hound was so good at getting the raccoon!

I'd tell you more about my old pack mates—all their names and exact breeds, how old they were, what each one liked and didn't like, what they were good at, the stories they told—except that I'm pretty sure I'll never see any of them again. That's life, but it still made me angry.

Those farm humans left me locked in a cage with nothing to eat or drink. Thinking what would have happened if the animal shelter hadn't found me made me angrier still. That's how trustworthy and grateful humans are: not much at all. New humans had taken me, but they wanted me to sleep in a cage.

No way. No how. Not happening.

Chapter 7: Lido

Houses were giving way to small shops crowded together. Lido's fear came true: he couldn't see Jal. His trainee had chased the extra-fast Chihuahua around a corner. He could still smell Jal's scent, though. It lingered in the air as he, Skil, and Nygin ran by. Lido could also still hear the little dog taunting the three-month-old Collie who was already bigger than him.

"Ha ha! You can't even catch me!"

"You're too clumsy!"

"You're slow!"

"Some big Kaxian you are!"

Lido knew what the super-fast Nique was up to. He knew exactly what he was doing. He would lead Jal into some kind of trouble so that the humans called the animal shelter to come get Jal. Lido couldn't let that happen. The pack had trusted Lido and put him in charge of Jal. Lido had to rescue Jal from those pesky Niques and their meddling.

At the corner where his nose told him that Jal and the Nique had turned, the smell of all kinds of plants that humans eat greeted Lido: potatoes, carrots, celery, strawberries, onions, broccoli, apples, oranges… There was also the familiar scent of red grapes that might even be from the vineyard where he and Skil lived.

To his right, there in the distance, he saw Jal!

Impossibly, the super-fast Nique was just as far ahead of Jal as he had been when he first gave chase. They were still running. That Nique was running impossibly fast.

Lido led Skil and Nygin around the corner, and a bunch of humans came into view. They were all in the street. It was blocked by a barricade so no cars could get in. The humans were gathered in clumps around tables full of the plants humans eat. The whole area was sheltered from the sun by cloth stretched out on poles supported by flimsy stands.

"Oh no," Skil said behind him.

"Jal!" Lido yelled. "Jal! Come back here! Quit chasing that Nique! He's trying to get you in trouble with the humans!"

It was no use. The Nique was good at his job. He kept up the taunting.

"Run, run, run, little Kaxian!"

"Doesn't your mommy feed you enough?"

"You aren't very strong!"

"You can't even catch me!"

Lido was amazed. Jal easily should have caught the Chihuahua by now. What was making him run so fast? It must be some new Nique technology. That was not good. He made a mental note to tell Heg and Koog about that when he got back to the mine later.

The Chihuahua was entering the area with all the humans and tables and poles on flimsy stands and piles of plants that humans eat. Being so small, he easily ran between the humans' legs to get under the tables full of plants. Once under there, he began telling the humans lies.

The humans couldn't understand him, of course, but the humans were smart enough to understand the gist of it from the way the Nique said it. He would pick a human to run out from under the table to and bark at for a second before he ran back under the table. It was very effective at getting the humans to listen to the Nique. Kax on him!

"Humans! Help me! I need you, Humans!"

"I was minding my own business when these big dogs started chasing me!"

"Help! I'm little and defenseless!"

"These big dogs are after me for no reason!"

Every bit of that was a lie!

Lido felt himself growing angry at the Nique for his lies. He knew better. He knew the Nique was trying to make him mad so that he couldn't think straight. Lido also knew that Jal wasn't nearly as aware of what was going on. Lido was sure that Heg had told Jal and the other recruits to just run on by if the Niques taunted the Kaxians, hadn't he? Hadn't their parents told them that, too?

But Lido was older and knew it took experience to just ignore taunting.

"Oh no!" Skil said again.

The three Yorkshire Terrier Niques had caught up now. The four Niques were running as close to the humans as they could, even under the humans' legs, if possible. Jal couldn't fit under the humans' legs. He would knock the humans over if he tried to chase the Niques through there.

Desperately, Lido called out again.

"Jal! Come here! Stop chasing the Niques!"

Jal didn't listen.

Lido knew the young pup must be in a hunting

frenzy, so intent on his prey that he didn't even hear his own name being called. It made him mad at himself for not going over the rules enough before they set out on their scouting patrol. Puppies simply had to know better than to chase the Niques. But that couldn't help him now.

Falling for the Niques' ploy, Jal doggedly followed the Chihuahua Nique, even when doing so caused a human to trip over him.

"Ooh!" Skil said.

She was cringing. Lido knew she feared what might happen to the human and how angry that would make all the humans get at Jal.

Fortunately, no one got hurt.

Unfortunately, Jal caused a scene.

The human who tripped was carrying a large load of potatoes. He dropped them and grabbed for anything that would help him steady himself. He grabbed one of the poles that held the cloth sunshades up.

The pole was only supported by a flimsy stand. It wobbled back and forth, making the whole block's cloth sunshade wave around like it was dancing.

The potatoes rolled around on the ground as if they were trying to trip the humans.

Some of the humans did trip over the potatoes, and they, too, grabbed for whatever they could reach that might help them keep their balance.

More sun-shader support poles were loosened from their flimsy stands.

The sun-shader danced even more wildly.

Instead of running to get away from the trouble they had caused, the Niques circled back around and ran through the same area again!

Still oblivious to the danger of the humans' anger, Jal kept on chasing the Chihuahua Nique through humans' legs and under tables full of human-food plants.

Now having enough time to realize what was happening, the humans started reacting.

"Get away from here, you mangy dogs!"

"Leave those little dogs alone, you big bully!"

"Shoo! Shoo! Go away, you pests!"

Lido, Skil, and Nygin arrived on the scene just as the humans had started shooing Jal and the little dogs away. Lido figured the Niques had planned it this way, making it most likely the Kaxians would take the blame for the chaos, when, as usual, the Niques had provoked them.

Lido called Skil and Nygin into a small sheltered area out of the humans' sight behind a parked car.

"Skil! Nygin! Over here!"

They came to him right away, much to Lido's relief. He tried a voice command on Jal one last time.

"Jal! Scout recruit Jal! Come here!"

But Jal just kept on chasing the extra-fast Nique round and round a table full of mulberries. The Nique kept going out of its way to go between humans' legs. They were going faster now. The humans had to jump out of the way to grab the flimsy poles and keep from falling.

Kids started grabbing the poles and swinging on them, even if they weren't falling.

Some of the humans grabbed at the dogs as they ran by, and one boy almost caught Jal.

One man took out his cell phone, dialed a number, and started speaking urgently.

"Connect me to the dog catcher, please!"

Skil gasped. "Did you hear that, Lido?"

Lido's tail did something it hadn't done in almost a year. It went under his belly.

"Yeah, I know" Lido said. "He's calling animal control."

Nygin peed a little, she was so afraid of the dog catcher.

Lido needed help. He needed more help than Skil and Nygin could give him. He prided himself on being a good scout trainer and a great defender, but he had to admit he'd completely lost control of the situation.

In a quiet, indoor voice, Lido said, "When all else fails, follow directions."

Skil ginned at him.

Lido grinned back at his mate. His tail came out from under his belly. He looked at it and then back at Skil

She licked his face.

He looked into her loving eyes, sighed, and shook his head slowly. Then he looked Nygin and Skil in the eyes by turns.

"Who am I to get angry at Jal? I haven't been following my orders, either. I should have asked Kax for help the moment Jal started chasing the Niques."

Nygin shrugged and looked confused. Poor girl. He shouldn't have let her see him this way. She needed him to be strong so that she knew she could follow his lead.

In her indoor voice, Skil said, "Chin up. It's not too late. Let's all three ask Kax for help right now. Three are better than one!"

Lido smiled at his beautiful mate and licked her face.

Nygin smiled and looked more content, now that they were back on familiar ground.

The three Kaxians huddled together and quietly appealed to Kax in their minds, keeping their eyes open for an opportunity to stop the chaos the Niques were causing.

Meanwhile, back outside their shelter at the Farmers' Market, the sun-shader gave way and floated down, covering the humans' eyes.

One of the humans tripped over a potato and fell into a cart full of apples.

This upset the apple cart enough that it fell over, spilling a hundred apples all over the ground and sending them rolling everywhere along with the potatoes.

Even Jal tripped over one of the apples. He skidded out and fell onto his side.

The instant Jal stopped running, Skil ran over, grabbed him by the scruff of his neck, and carried him over behind the parked car where Lido and Nygin watched, impressed.

Seeing that his party was once again whole, Lido lead them away from the area where, thanks to the Niques, the humans were expecting the dog catcher to arrive at any minute.

***

Back at the Kaxian jex mine, Lido reported everything that had happened. He didn't leave out any part of it. He took full responsibility for not appealing to Kax about Jal's chase as soon as it started.

Heg and Koog looked extra serious when Lido and Skil told what they had witnessed about the Nique being able to run extra fast.

"The Chihuahua ran extra fast?" Heg asked,

looking at Lido sideways with his eyebrows lowered.

"Yep, the Chihuahua," Lido said, nodding.

"Wow, that's got to be some new Nique technology. It's going to be trouble!" Koog said, his eyes open wide.

Lido noticed something then that scared him more than when that human had called the dog catcher. He noticed that his strong leader Koog's tail was under his belly and shaking, like a scared little puppy's.

"You know it," Heg said. His tail was under his belly and shaking, too.

***

A little later, Heg took Jal and Lido into an empty side cave. Once they were alone, he looked at Jal sternly.

"Do you understand what almost happened because you disobeyed orders?"

Jal rolled over onto his back, exposing his belly to Heg's teeth and letting Heg know that Jal knew Heg was boss.

While Jal couldn't see, Heg raised his eyes to Lido for a moment.

Lido started to roll over onto his back, too.

Heg nosed Lido back up, but gave him a stern look.

Lido lowered his head to Heg.

Heg nosed Lido up just before he nosed Jal up.

Heg said, "Well, Jal? What almost happened?"

"I almost went to the animal shelter."

Jal's voice was shaky, and his tail was under his belly.

"That's right, Jal. Skil saved you just in time. Next time, Kax might not be so willing to get you out of the fix you put yourself in. Can we trust you to obey orders from now on?"

Jal's ears perked up.

"You mean, I'm still a defender? I still get to serve the pack?"

Jal's tail came out from under his belly and started tentatively waving.

Heg stepped forward, rested his head on top of Jal's head, looked into Lido's eyes, and addressed them both without Jal seeing.

"You might be taking a break from being a defender, but yes, you still get to serve the pack."

Chapter 8: Oreo

My nose caught fresh wolf scent when I'd been going up the mountain above the watered green desert suburb for a few hours. I stood there a minute, letting my nose sniff out how many different wolves were up here claiming this territory.

Yes, urine was the main thing I was smelling. I could smell it from a long ways away, and for a long time after it had been left. I could also tell how far away it was, and how long it had been there. If you were a dog, then you'd sniff urine, too. Yes, you would.

There were the lovely scents of three wolf ladies of childbearing age. My nose enjoyed their scents. One was quite close. The others were more distant right now, but often close. I smelled one distant elderly lady wolf. My nose also told me there were 6 fully grown male wolves around this part of the mountain often, and that one of these was quite close right now.

Yikes! This was a large pack of 14 wolves up here, claiming this territory. Of the 14, 4 were just puppies, barely weaned, not threats. That left 10, each very much a threat.

My tail did that scared puppy thing where it hides under my belly and shakes really fast, but I deliberately pulled it out and made it stay up. My ears also wanted to go down in fright, but I made them stay up, too. I pulled my ears up mostly so I could hear better. Yeah, that was why.

Are you wondering how I knew it was wolves and not other dogs?

There is no mistaking wolf scent for dog scent, if you have a nose as keen as a dog's nose. Sure, I could see how you humans might think the two scents were alike, but trust me, they are not the same.

Dog scent is civilized.

It's always mixed with human scent and the scent of things humans have made: soap, perfume, dog food... Oh, some dogs are hunters, yes, but we are nowhere near wild. We've been living with humans for thousands of years. They have bred all the wildness out of us. Without being taught, most of us wouldn't live a week if left out in the wilderness without humans to care for us. Almost none of us would live if left out in the wilderness alone, like I was now.

Dogs are tame.

Wolves are wild.

They are independent and self-reliant: scornful of cities, civilization and human ways—fiercely independent, I should have said. Even the wolves in cages. Especially the wolves in cages.

Don't get near a wolf. They bite.

I should have turned my tail the other way and run down the mountain right then, but I didn't. I stayed there near the top of the mountain I had been climbing for two hours. My nose was up, and I just kept sniffing the air, not wanting to turn and run.

Yes, I was afraid of the wolves.

I knew they would come chase me off their

territory, at the very least. Two would always stay back to guard the 4 puppies, but that left 8 who would come hunt me in a pack. I knew that I would have slim-to-no chance against a pack of 8 wolves, out here on my own.

Did I tell you hunting in a pack is easy and fun?

I was sure the wolves found it so as well.

Yes, I was so afraid, I was shaking. My tail kept trying to go under my belly, and my ears kept trying to fold down. It would have made sense for me to turn tail and run back down the mountain into the suburbs again. Back to the humans and their uptight dog. Back to safety.

I was more afraid of the cage, though.

I was even a little angry that the new humans had tried to put me in a cage again. Out here in the wild, I could hunt for my dinner. I couldn't hunt in a cage.

I shook myself, trying to stop being afraid. I was happy to remain angry. Anger is more fun than fear, so we often talk ourselves into being angry when we're scared.

Survival instinct kicked in.

Instinct told me that if I wasn't going down where the humans lived, down to civilization where the wolves wouldn't go, down where every bit of common sense told me I should be going... If I was going to be stubborn and stay up here in the wolves' territory, then I should at least find a high place where I could put my back against a rock while I slept.

I went up, up, up, to the top of the mountain, stopping only to drink where a little trickle of water filled a small puddle in a canyon. The wolf scent was particularly strong there, but hey, I was thirsty.

At the top of the mountain, there was snow. My

nose was cold up there, but the rest of me is covered in fur so thick I can be in the water long enough to catch a duck without getting my skin wet. The temperature up there suited me just fine. I tried to convince myself I preferred the temperature up there to the way those humans kept their den so hot inside that it always made me pant. That didn't work, so I went back to being mad at them about the cage.

I found a nice rock to put my back against, gazed up, and had my mind swallowed by how starry the night sky was, up there.

There were so many stars, I could have counted all night and not gotten them all. The longer I stared at the stars, the more I saw, too. What seemed at first to be a single star would turn out to be a cluster of them. This happened over and over until I felt overwhelmed by how big space must be.

My fear and anger receded.

My mind must have started to drift.

Even though I was awake, I had the strangest dream.

I was shooting through space toward a particular star. I wasn't in a spaceship. It was just me in my fur, going so fast that my fur was flat against me with the wind. OK, yeah, there's probably no wind in space because there's no atmosphere, but this was my dream, so it had wind.

It wasn't scary, more like a fun ride down a snowy hill. A bunch of star clusters whizzed by me, as well as spiral formations of other stars and many gassy space nebula shaded in pink, purple, red, and blue.

As I zoomed in close to that one particular star, I noticed planets circling it. One of those planets rushed up to me. I seemed to land on that planet! In outer space! This was my dream, so I could breathe the air on this foreign planet just fine, and I didn't even worry that I might not be able to. Of course I could.

I saw a city not far away. It was a dream, so it only took a second to run there.

Everyone in the city was a dog! What's more, they were all large dogs. There were no small dogs in sight. Huh.

Dogs were running up and down paved streets, coming in and out of homes and shops using little paw-print pads that opened the doors, and stopping to talk to each other by the sides of the streets. They wagged their tails and nosed each other. They were happy.

Sounds caught my ear from above. When I looked up, I blinked and shook my head. There were many airplanes up above my head, but not far above. And dogs were flying them! The large dogs landed their airplanes on the tops of the skyscraper buildings, got out, clicked their remotes to lock their airplane doors, and then trotted over to the building doors up top.

My vision followed one of these dogs inside what my mind told me was his den, up on top of a skyscraper. It was made of some kind of stone that resembled human cement. It also was more similar to the humans' dens than to a wolf den, being built above the ground. Inside, the floor was covered not unlike the floor inside the humans' dens.

But everything was made for dogs.

There were objects that had shiny lights on them, sort of like the humans used. My paw would have fit into the holes the dogs used to make the lights shine and to make the objects work. Other objects cooked food for the dogs and bathed the dogs. They had soft fluffy beds to sleep on, with massage built in that they could control with their paw pads. The dog had a brushing machine that fluffed him up and scratched his back and got all the grass out of his fur. His puppies had a machine that played with them, acting like prey animals they would hunt all over their den.

The dogs had TVs and computers, refrigerators, showers, and pretty much all the fancy stuff that humans had inside their dens, but it was all made for dogs and operated with dog paws!

I wanted to stay and see more, but before I knew what was happening, I zoomed away from that planet, away from that star, past a bunch more star clusters, spiral galaxies, and nebula, toward another particular star. This one had planets, too, and again I landed on a particular planet.

This one was similar to the first in that everyone was a dog and everything was built for dogs to use. These dogs flew airplanes, too, and had dog shops, dog homes, and dog streets. The only difference was—all these dogs were small.

For a brief moment, I woke up back on top of the mountain with my back to the rock, just staring up at the starry sky.

And then I was high up in the air, watching as the sun went around the wrong way and all the cities disappeared. All the roads disappeared, too, and the train tracks. Even the farms disappeared. All around were just plants and rocks. This long ago, nothing human-made could be seen from way up in the air.

It was a dream, so I was back on the ground in less than a second.

A loud roaring noise hurt my ears, and a bright

light made me close my eyes.

When I opened them, I knew I was still dreaming because I saw something that looked like that RV I'd seen a ways back down the mountain, only much bigger. It flew down to the ground from way up in the sky and landed. Its doors opened, and hundreds of big dogs came out. And then the huge RV sank down into the ground and disappeared from sight, but I knew it was still there. I saw other RVs land all around the world, let their dogs out, and then sink underground and hide.

Then I was up in the air again, watching all the big dogs spread out and befriend humans. The way you know things in dreams that you wouldn't know in real life, I knew that it was taking years for all the dogs to befriend their humans. I knew I was seeing highlights here and there and getting the big picture of what was going on.

I saw wolves with angry faces on the mountains, staring down at the big dogs.

While the humans worked, the puppies of the big dogs left to dig in the ground together. They dug up something and brought it to the RVs up in the hills, where two dogs waited to take it from them and blast off, to take it where huge RVs waited, up in space. They took it to the first planet I had seen. The dogs there used it. It was vital to them. They wouldn't have all these wonders of airplanes, RVs, skyscrapers, and comfort without this stuff that puppies dug out of the ground, here on Earth.

Something tugged at my mind about those RV-type things up in the hills. Did they remind me of something I had seen? I was sure I was close to figuring it out.

Then there was another loud noise and another bright light that made me close my eyes.

Smaller huge RV-type things of a different color and shape had landed.

And little dogs came out of them.

The little dogs showed up at the big dogs' holes in the ground, demanding they be given some of the stuff the big dogs had dug up. Jex, the stuff was called.

"Go find your own planet to mine!" the big dogs told the little dogs. "We were here first!"

The little dogs said, "There is plenty for all of us! You need to share it!"

"No. The jex on Earth is ours."

"You'll share it with us one way or another."

"Whatever we do, no humans can know that dogs are aliens. They are bigger than both of us," the big dogs said.

"Agreed," said the little dogs.

Chapter 9: Belg

Belg crept up a ravine, as usual keeping his nose open to all that lurked and flew around him: rats, rabbits, squirrels, voles, raccoons, snakes, lizards, quail, blue jays, pigeons... and old traces of mountain lions, bears and other threats.

With just the quarter moon's glow, he had no trouble seeing anything, particularly small prey animals that moved quickly. If the moon were full, then he would be able to see even better at night than in the daytime. His vision was perfect for hunting at night. A reflective layer inside his retinas, the tapetum, made it so.

Belg stopped, waiting in a silent crouch, his hindquarters jiggling a little in anticipation.

A human might say Belg had trouble distinguishing red from green, but he had little need to do that. He ate mostly meat. He might eat berries if nothing else were available, but his nose told him where the berries were, amid the greenery. He didn't need his eyes to do that.

Belg continued dilating his nostrils, taking in all the scents but concentrating on one in particular.

And anyway, smell was Belg's main sense, not sight. He could smell every creature within almost two miles of him. Not only that, he could smell traces they had left behind, and he could tell how long ago they'd been there. He could also tell which direction his prey was moving, and how fast. And how close he was getting, moving toward his meal.

Belg turned his head toward the scent. He needed his eyes on the creature for this last part.

Despite what Neya thought, Belg was not lazy. He could have stood outside the cave with his nose open and known enough to keep guard over her and the pups, but he had orders, and he followed them. He circled the cave for a mile radius around it, checking a wider radius for any scent of intruders.

There, under that sagebrush in the shadow of the pine boughs. Shadows that moved against the wind. It was the squirrel he'd been following for a minute with his nose. His dinner.

Belg crept up on the squirrel, not unlike how a cat creeps up on the string you drag for it. His body low to the ground, he didn't make any sound to tell the squirrel, "Be afraid." His ears continued to pan around, alert for anything telling Belg, himself, "Be afraid." His tail wagged behind him, giving away his enjoyment of his task.

His claws dug into the dirt, giving him purchase to pounce.

Bam!

Belg grabbed the squirrel with his teeth and ate it whole in less than ten seconds, leaving nothing behind. Wasting nothing.

He wouldn't hunt larger prey alone, but the pack sometimes brought down an animal bigger than they could eat at one meal. They ate the most nutritious parts first and saved the rest for tomorrow, under some ice or snow if possible. In a lake or stream otherwise. Of course, they brought a meal home for the puppies and for the scout and the nanny wolf. That was as much as they could carry in their mouths.

Wait.

What was that?

Belg stopped running on the top of a rise. Silhouetted against the moon, the wolf raised his nose up to catch the swiftest wind.

He dilated his nostrils over and over to bring the wind into his nose so he would catch a whiff of every scent passing by in the air.

There it was again.

He smelled an off scent that didn't quite belong in nature. He knew what it was, but only because the scent had been taught to him, using samples from sticks brought up from the trails farther down the mountain.

The dog aliens usually didn't come up this far, especially not at night. They usually weren't a threat, either, but it was his duty to investigate. How many were up here? What was their intent?

If the aliens were looking to hunt, sleep, drink, or otherwise encroach on the pack's territory, then his duty was to help make sure they didn't. The dog aliens were a menace to native Earth kind. He snickered. The big dog aliens were a menace. The little dog aliens were just funny. This scent was the big, menacing variety.

If he handled this right, then Scur might take him hunting next time. Hunting sounded much more fun than scouting. Anything did. Well, anything except nannying. Poor Neya.

Finally, something exciting is happening on this patrol!

Oh, those deer were fun.

But aliens!

At the thought of encountering a dog alien menace, all of Belg's fur bristled, making him look twice his size. His ears went straight up and pivoted every which way, seeking out the sound of his new prey. His tail went high in the air to help him balance if he had to run. His claws gripped the ground to help him run faster or fight better. His nostrils dilated to keep him informed of his enemy's location.

His enemy smelled like fear.

Taking extra care to be silent, Belg went toward the new scent.

He found a set of alien paw tracks near the cave. Before they went up the mountain, they went right up to the pack's water.

A filthy alien drank our water!

Killing something as big as an alien outside the safety of the pack was forbidden, but he should get a close sample of the scent so he could share it with his pack. That would help the rest of them find the alien. Yeah. That was why he simply had to get a look at it.

He followed the alien tracks up the mountain.

They stopped because the mountain got rocky, but his nose told him where to go. Finally, his ears told him the alien was asleep just around the next boulder.

This is the type of excitement I want in my days!

He crept around the corner for a look at the alien.

It lay curled up against the far rock sleeping, not three feet from him. Its black and white speckled coat oddly helped to hide it in the moonlight. It was about his same size and build, but not nearly as fit as he was.

It's been lying around all the time, the lazy thing. I guess all the running I do as a scout is good for something. I could take it. Easily.

Belg imagined himself lunging at the alien…

But they forbid me to hunt large prey alone.

I'm not hunting, though! This is a scouting mission. I'm just getting a scent sample. May as well make it a good one!

All in one motion, Belg lunged forward, bit the alien's ear, and was on his way back down the mountain. Its ear tasted a bit like coyote. He wanted more, but obedience had been drilled into him. Obeying orders came to him sooner than not. Anyway, he knew the pack would take care that the alien didn't invade their territory. He also instinctively understood that hunting it with the whole pack was safer.

Also, he knew the pack would hurt him if he disobeyed.

He ran down to the cave and rushed inside to warn Neya.

"Stay in the cave, and keep all the pups inside. There's an alien close by. I'm going to alert the pack. I'll be out front, but be on your guard, just in case."

He rushed back out and howled to the pack.

"Alien! Peak! Slept and drank here!"

Hoping the alien showed up and gave him an excuse to attack before he heard the reply, he trained his eyes on the way he'd just come down, while his howl echoed around the canyons for a few seconds.

"On our way! Do not chase! Stay and guard the pups!"

Sighing, Belg acknowledged the alpha's command.

"Guarding!"

While he waited for the pack to return, he kept his eye out, still hoping the alien came down this way so he could attack it before the others arrived. As part of his guard duties, he would attack, not because he wanted to. He would have no choice. He had to defend the puppies. Yes he did.

The moon did not grace him with that opportunity.

Porl the old scout showed up first, defending the alphas by staying between them and the unknown that lay ahead of the pack. Porl's snout was graying. He was the second-oldest pack member. He eyed Belg, making sure the younger scout was doing his duty properly.

The alphas, Scur and Fleek, showed up next. They both had confidence in their gaze when they met Belg's eyes. They checked on him only briefly. He could tell they were thinking about how to most quickly rid the pack of the alien menace. The two of them were most of the pack's parents.

Belg's litter mates Ordn, Tolt, and Kess followed directly behind the alphas. The youngest hunters, they were also the strongest fighters. Ordn guarded the alphas' right side, Tolt their left, and Kess stayed directly between his parents and whatever might come up behind them.

Anything coming up behind the alphas would first need to eat up the stragglers, Fulm and Old Ega, who came in last.

Maybe after this is over, I'll challenge Ega for the right to be a hunter. She might even just let me win. She has to know I'm stronger than she is now. Yeah, she has more experience, but whoever's stronger usually wins a challenge.

After a few seconds, Belg realized that Ega's eyes were staring right back at him.

Wow. I guess she knows what I plan to do. Got to be careful how I stare at older wolves.

Belg shook himself just as his father, Scur the alpha male, arrived in front of him.

Scur's fir was just as bristled as Belg's. All of the wolves' fur was. They all wanted to hunt the alien. Scur stood tall and proud in front of him, blinking, but Belg could see that Scur's mind was already in the hunt.

"Good job getting a scent sample and then calling us, Belg. I smell where the alien went. Stay here and guard the pups. We'll make sure it no longer infringes on our territory."

What? He was being told to stay here? But he was the one who alerted them to the alien threat! Belg thought he should be allowed to go along and make sure that threat was removed.

"Aw! Can't Ega stay here? I found the alien! I should get to go hunt it!" The next thing Belg knew, he was on his back with Porl's teeth at his throat.

Kess ran up and licked Porl's face, then did a somersault, but in a sloppy way so that she landed sideways and went rolling off in an awkward way. Ordn, Tolt, and Fleek laughed. Scur even grinned a little. Kess was doing a good job keeping the pack members from hurting each other, and that was her job as jester, besides being a hunter.

Porl loosened his hold on Belg's neck to watch Kess's somersault, but just a little.

Scur's voice came from outside Belg's vision. "Porl, stay here with Belg to make sure he guards the pups as he was told."

Porl grunted his agreement, his teeth still on Belg's throat.

Still angry, now Belg was embarrassed, too. *I guess disobeying Scur's orders is not going to give me my chance to challenge Ega.* Ultimately, fear for his life made his survival instinct kick in, which dominated his response. He relaxed and quit struggling.

Porl let go of Belg's throat and nudged him up with his nose.

Scur gestured to Fulm to go first and follow the alien's scent.

Fleek gazed briefly at the cave and sniffed, but seeming satisfied that her pups would be fine in her absence a little while longer, she followed Fulm.

The pack rushed off after the alien, leaving Belg behind with Porl and Neya, to care for the pups.

Chapter 10: Neya

Belg came rushing into the cave. The moon and stars shining in from outside gave Neya enough light to see that his fur was all bristled up and his teeth were exposed. He must have been close to getting into a fight. A part of her was proud of him for obeying the order not to fight or hunt large animals without the rest of the pack.

Between deep breaths, he spoke to her with the authority of a scout, even though she used to be his nanny, too.

"Stay in the cave, and keep all the pups inside. There's an alien close by. I'm going to alert the pack. I'll be out front, but be on your guard, just in case."

Another part of Neya, the larger part, was overcome with a longing that she thought had died. A love she thought she was over. A hope she had given up on.

Her ears heard what Belg said. They told her body, which told her head to nod at him so he would know she'd heard what he said. Her head nodded.

Belg rushed back outside the cave and started howling to the pack about the alien near their cave. The pack howled back that they were coming and ordered Belg to wait for them.

The pack would be here soon. She would be relieved of her constant duty to feed and water and clean up after the pups. She should be looking forward to that and wagging her tail in happiness. She knew that.

But Neya remained in a daze.

Her memories took her back to a year ago when she'd met a handsome alien in a dream. She'd known he was an alien, but he'd been kind, playful, and fun. She'd seen their whole lives together in the brief duration of that dream. They'd had pups together and been happy. She'd been quite smitten with him, and had expected him to show up as a lone wolf would, to claim her as his mate. It had been a strong urge, to go with him when he came.

The urge had suddenly vanished a few days after she met Clem, and she hadn't thought of it until now. She sat there dazed for a few moments, dumbstruck at how vivid and powerful her memories of Clem were.

Neya had barely noticed the primary alien scent Belg brought into their cave. She was hung up on the faint whiff of Clem's scent that came with this new alien's scent. The arrival of the two alien scents together made her feel like helping this new alien, for the sake of the other, her brief forbidden love.

She considered the puppies who were in her care. If she could make them go to sleep, then she would be free to reach out to Clem in her mind.

She said, "It's time for the story of Elat and the sheep. Do you know that story?"

Glar wagged his tail the way he always did when she announced a story. "No."

"No," Stulp said, cuddling up to Neya and smiling up at her with tongue hanging out of her mouth.

"Nuh uh." Filp still stalked his cricket between

the cracks of the cave wall, his tail wagging slowly in concentration.

Little Crom cuddled up to Neya next to Stulp. "Nope. Yay! A new story!"

Neya started the story.

"Elat was a scout like Wall and Belg, but his job was to keep track of the sheep that wandered near his pack's land. Do you know what sheep are, Crom?"

"They're good to eat!"

"Yes, they are. What else do you know about sheep, Glar?"

"They're white and puffy."

"That's right. Filp, let the cricket rest. Come on over here and lie down."

Filp hung his head. "Do I have to?"

Neya looked at Filp sideways.

"OK." Filp lay down next to Stulp.

"Get comfortable, puppies. This is a long story. Come curl up next to your Neya, Glar."

Glar lay down on the other side of Crom.

All the puppies curled up and got comfortable.

Neya licked each one's head a few times, to help them relax. They all folded back their ears and rose their heads toward her tongue after her first lick, to encourage her to lick them some more.

Neya continued the story.

"Elat had a whole field of fluffy white sheep to watch and keep track of. He did this by counting. As each sheep passed by, he counted it. Let's help Elat count his sheep. All together now: one, two, three, four, five…"

After they counted to forty, Neya gazed at the puppies. Reassuring herself that they slept, she stretched out next to them so that if they woke, she would be alerted.

Will this work? I have to try it.

Neya wanted to be in the vision state that she vaguely recalled from her encounter with the handsome alien. She wanted to contact him again. To warn him that her pack were hunting the other alien, the one who had brought his scent to her.

How did I get there before? Think!

It came to her. She had been daydreaming. Daydreaming about leaving the cave and going on an adventure.

Once again, in her imagination, Neya pictured herself leaving the cave, alone, in the daytime. She saw the path down the mountain to a meadow, and why not make it spring? The meadow was green with spring grass, and flowers bloomed. The creek was high, and it chortled with water.

A few sheep ran through the meadow.

Neya giggled.

And then she got down to the business she came here to conduct.

Clem? Are you here? Your friend who smells like this… She brought out the primary scent Belg had brought into the cave with him, the scent connected with Clem's own scent. *He's in trouble! Clem?*

There he was! There was Clem the dog alien. Just as handsome as before. Running toward her across the meadow with his tail wagging high in the air and his ears perked up. He had grown quite a bit since she first saw him a year ago. His barrel chest was larger than hers, his back a bit higher than hers. His legs were taller and skinnier than hers. She imagined he could out-run her. All in all, the two of them were the same size, she figured.

Unable to help herself, she thought back on the year since she'd met him. The scene changed so that the two of them were floating like ghosts on the inside of the cave, watching Nanny Neya care for the wolf pups. Often, she looked up to see if Clem had come to claim her as his mate. Her thoughts came to him all on their own, as if she were trying to tell him about her yearning to leave her role as pack nanny and start a family of her own.

That was when she realized she was no longer counting on him being the father of that family and the alpha male of the new pack it would form.

That's odd. Clem, I'm no longer sure you will be the 'lone wolf' who comes to claim me and take me away from all this. You seem like you're already taken. Have you taken a mate? I don't smell a mate, only humans and your friend.

Clem arrived by her side and smiled at her, his tail still wagging.

"Hello, Neya."

They smiled at each other for a moment, but it wasn't the moment she'd been waiting for, all these months. It wasn't a reunion. It was just a conversation they would have and then both be on their separate ways. She could tell all this the moment she saw Clem.

He said, "No, I haven't taken a mate. But it is something similar to that. I've bonded with my humans. I am no longer free to leave them. I must obey their commands, which include staying with them and not letting my new friend, whom they call my 'baby brother,' run away."

She said, "That's a full load! Are you happy?"

"Yes. I love my humans, and they love me. They call me Raffle, and that is the name I go by, now."

Neya saw his memories then, Raffle with his two humans, a male and a female. The humans looking on him lovingly and petting him. Them walking with Raffle on a leash in their neighborhood and in a nearby park with him loose and dozens of other dogs running loose with him, playing. Them tucking him into his bed at night by the side of their bed. Them giving him treats from their plates. She could tell he did love his humans, and she was glad they loved him back. She was happy for him. She was.

Raffle's tail stopped wagging, and his ears drooped a little.

"Besides, Neya, the male alpha of your new pack needs to be a hunter. I'm a herder."

They smiled at each other, tails wagging slowly, saying goodbye to what could have been, but wasn't meant to be.

And then he broke the moment and asked the question she had called him here to answer. "My humans call that alien my 'baby brother.' Do you know where he is?"

Neya nodded. Getting an idea, she closed her eyes and pictured the top of her pack's mountain in her mind. When she opened her eyes in the vision state, she and Raffle were up there, in the vision.

"Your 'baby brother' was here when Belg bit his ear. Belg went down this way, so Baby Brother must have gone down over on that side."

Neya concentrated and made them both zoom extra fast down the trail Raffle's baby brother had followed, almost all the way down the other side of the mountain. She stopped them just past the next Kaxian space shuttle.

She looked at him sadly. "This is where your

friend is going, and how far he'll get before they catch up with him. My pack is after him. He had a good head start while they returned from hunting, but they will catch up with him before he gets back to the safety of the human civilization. You need to send him help. I imagine you can."

"Thank you, Neya. I will send you help, too, if I find any for you. Goodbye." Raffle turned and started running down the mountain, and then he disappeared.

Neya woke up in the cave. She panicked for a second. Had Belg checked in on the puppies? Had he realized she was gone?

She checked on the puppies. They were all still pressed up next to her, snoring away. Whew. She hadn't known how worried she was about them until she'd woken up.

Thinking back on her adventures with Raffle and her conversation with him, Neya realized this time had been just like the last time she'd met with the dog alien: she hadn't really moved away from the cave at all. Their adventures and their talk had all been just in her mind, sort of like a dream.

But she felt sure it hadn't been just a dream, that she really had warned Raffle about her pack going to attack his adopted brother. She also realized she wasn't worried about the outcome. Her confidence in Raffle's ability to handle the situation surprised her.

Neya shook herself so she could snap out of this odd dream state.

She heard the pack members talking outside.

The puppies woke up with Neya's shake, and then they heard the pack outside, too.

"The pack is back!"

"Where is our new meat?"

"Momma, where are you?"

"Daddy, are you here?"

Neya went to the cave entrance, but their parents, Scur and Fleek, were just leaving with most of the pack. Hearing that Porl was to stay behind and make sure Belg obeyed orders amused her briefly. She turned to the puppies.

"The pack has gone back out hunting. There is no new meat yet."

"Aw!"

"Why?"

"I'm sure they'll bring meat when they come back this time. Let's all go back to sleep so that seems like it happens sooner, OK?"

They all lay back down. Neya licked their heads to soothe them.

For another minute, Neya felt very attached to Raffle, and sad because of the family she would no longer have with him. Gradually, her sadness turned into confusion.

He'll send me help? But I don't need any help.

But as she looked at her sleeping brothers and sisters and once again wished she could have puppies of her own, the thought of getting help gave Neya a new hope.

Chapter 11: Lido

With his head still resting on Jal's head, Heg winked at Lido.

Lido shook his head, thinking he had imagined it.

Heg nosed Jal. "Scoot on out and see what Koog is telling the pack, Jal."

"OK! Sorry I ran off, Lido, Skil. It won't happen again. I promise!"

"No worries, Jal. Be a good scout!"

"I will!"

Heg said, "Go ahead and call Skil in here. I have something to tell the two of you, and I think you'll like it." He smiled.

Lido ran into Koog's meeting, nosed Skil in the tummy, waited for her to look at him, and then nodded sideways toward the empty side cave where he'd met with Heg and Jal.

Skil wagged her tail and joined him in there.

"Hi, Skil! Momma to be!"

Skil lowered her head, and her tail went under her belly, but she slowly grinned at Heg. "Hi. You wanted to see me?"

Lido rubbed his back against his mate's back. "He wants to talk to both of us. Says we'll like it."

"Oh!" Skil's tail came out from under her belly and wagged.

Heg smiled at Skil first, and then at Lido. "I'm not happy that Jal disobeyed you, Lido, but I am glad you came in early. I was going to call you in early, anyway."

Lido blinked at Heg.

"Your parental leave from the mining operation starts tomorrow. Today was your last day as mining defenders."

Lido's ears went down, and his head lowered a bit. His tail stopped wagging.

Skil licked her mate's cheek.

Heg nosed Lido's chin up. "Aw, this is not bad news! You both have the most important job on this world in front of you: being parents to that litter of puppies that will be here in a few weeks!"

Lido looked at Skil. She was radiant with joy. He licked her cheek.

Heg's smile got even bigger. "Now come on, both of you! Follow me!"

Heg ran past the mining meeting room and up the tunnel to the outside.

Koog joined him.

Lido and Skil followed.

The four of them ran quite a ways, and as usual, Skil passed Lido up. She ran with Koog in the front, while Lido and Heg took up the rear.

"Where are we going?" Lido asked Heg.

"It's a surprise, but you should figure it out soon!"

When they ran past a house with a short white picket fence, Skil turned back and smiled at Lido.

His tail wagging wildly, Lido smiled back at Skil. "You're taking us to headquarters!"

"Yep." And then Heg smiled at him!

"I'm happy to go, but why?"

"It's half a party to celebrate your first litter and half an orientation to teach you new roles as Kaxian parents."

Lido and Skil smiled at each other even wider.

They ran up Headquarters Mountain, down into a valley, and into the dark of a cave. Down, down, down they ran: Lido, Skil, Heg, and Koog, their mining leader who was leading. The rest of the pack had stayed to guard their jex mine.

They arrived at Kaxian Headquarters.

A familiar computerized voice sounded out in Kanx.

"Identify."

Koog put his front paws up on two metal rocks and held his eyes open while the computer scanned the party and verified that no non-Kaxians were with them.

A metal door in what appeared to be the cave wall opened soundlessly to a dark room.

They all stepped inside onto the flat metal floor.

The metal door closed, and the light came on. Another door opened into a wide chamber that smelled of plastic and more metal.

"Surprise!"

Lido and Skil stood there grinning at more than a hundred Kaxian parents who weren't currently nursing litters, including both of their fathers, who ran to them and tackled them in loving affection.

"Dad! It's so great to see you!"

"Congratulations, Son!"

"Welcome to the parenting club, Skil!"

Their dads stayed with them for the rest of the party, nosing their heads every few seconds.

Next, all the Kaxians in the room came to congratulate the first-time expecting pair. The males butted noses with Lido while the females nuzzled noses with Skil.

As it was no doubt designed to, the gathering made Lido feel very proud and glad he had taken a mate and started a family. He met Skil's eyes, and they grinned at each other some more. Then curiosity got the better of him. He found Koog.

"Do you have a party here for every mated pair's first litter?"

"Yes, although after we eat, you'll see it is mostly training for you. Congratulations again, Lido!"

"We're going to eat?"

Koog just laughed and gestured with his nose to the front of the large room, where a Bull Mastiff that Lido recognized as one of the instructors at his miner's orientation faced the crowd.

"Please, sit."

The side conversations stopped instantly. Everyone turned to face the Bull Mastiff and sat down on the smooth metal floor.

"As most of you know and two of you will soon appreciate," he smiled at Lido and Skil, "Kax provides food from home for these special occasions. I hope you enjoy it, but also stop to think about how far away it came from, and remember your fellow Kaxians there who prepared it and sent it all the way here, with their love and congratulations."

Lido looked at Skil again.

"I didn't think we had any more hidden Kaxian memories."

"I didn't, either!"

As soon as he'd said, "love and congratulations,"

both of them had remembered the Kaxian duties that came with being Kaxian parents: teaching their puppies what it meant to be Kaxians and to commune with Kax.

They both felt great relief that the big mystery of parenthood was solved and now they could relax and enjoy their family life.

Skil grinned back at him, and then they ran together to enjoy the Pairing Feast that they each suddenly remembered they had partaken of thousands of times, for all the paired mates they each had known in all their past lives here on Earth.

To get to the Pairing Feast, they all took turns riding the three elevators down one level.

The food was brought out of a Kaxian kitchen where some dishes were chilled and others were heated up. There were 30 roasted Alpians, large prey animals from back home on Kax. They ate in a dining room that had many windows. Most of the windows had rock immediately on the other side of the glass, and only a few looked out any distance at all, and then just into very small, empty caves.

After the meal, everyone took turns riding the three elevators up two levels and then went into the theater to watch a parenting movie made on Kax. Lido remembered everything in it now, but he enjoyed the production, remembering there was a new movie at each such Feast. This one starred a new female, Taila Wagger, but he recognized the male, Sniffy Noser, from previous films.

When everyone else was busy watching the movie, Heg nosed Lido and Skil. When Lido looked at him, Heg pointed with his nose to a door. Lido and Skil followed him there.

Heg took them to a room with a bunch of computer monitors and paw pads. He turned one of these on, and a Kaxian official appeared on the screen.

"Hello, Lido, Skil. Love and congratulations. I'm Teemoosh, one of the council of governors here on Kax. Tell me all you saw of this new Nique speed technology. You first, Lido."

Lido said, "Thanks. Well, the one Nique, a Chihuahua, ran extra fast. We should have caught him, but he managed to stay in front of us and to lead my recruit into a trap."

Lido's eyebrows went together when he admitted this last part.

Teemoosh said, "Don't worry about the trap, Lido. Like you said, you should have been able to catch the Nique." Now he looked at Skil. "Could you tell how he was going so fast? Did he eat anything right before he took off?"

Skil said, "No, we didn't see him eat anything. One second they all were playing on the grass in front of their human, and the next second they were taunting the recruits, and then the fast one was running extra fast toward the trap."

Teemoosh said, "As you can imagine, we are very concerned about this new Nique speed technology. We're going to need spies to help us figure out how it works. I've already cleared it with Boss for you to be among them, if you two want the jobs."

Lido's chest puffed out and he stood up very straight.

Skil's tail wagged and she smiled really big.

Lido said, "We'll need to discuss it before we accept the jobs, but we're very flattered!"

Teemoosh said, "I understand. Don't take too long, though. I'll sign off now until you contact me later, Heg."

Heg said, "All right, Teemoosh," and he turned off the monitor. Then he spoke to Lido and Skil. "We'll leave you two alone for a minute so you can discuss this. I'm afraid that's all the time we can give you. We'll understand if either Lido or you don't accept the job, or both, but we need to offer it to someone else right away then."

Heg left the two of them alone, as he promised.

Lido and Skil looked at each other with big smiles on their faces.

She said, "I always thought it would be Raffle who got a big promotion like this!"

He said, "So I should take it?"

She said, "Of course you should! Should I?"

He said, "They know we're expecting puppies, so they must be giving you something you can do and still care for them. I say yes, but do what you want to, Skil."

She made a face, and then said, "I'm going to give someone else the chance. I want to concentrate on teaching our puppies how to be Kaxians. But you should go for it, Lido."

They smiled at each other.

When Heg came back in, they told him.

Heg smiled and pushed a paw pad, then said, "He took it, but she didn't. Do you want to come in and meet him?"

A male voice said, "Yeah, be right there."

Heg smiled at the two of them while they waited.

A really buff Pitt Bull Kaxian came in, and Heg introduced Lido to him.

"Eicks, this is Lido. Lido, this is Eicks, your new boss. This isn't goodbye, you guys. I'll still see you here whenever there's a new parent celebration!"

Eicks said, "Hello, Skil. Lido, let's trade scents so we can find each other if need be."

Lido moved forward and the two of them sniffed each other. Eicks told Lido to have a nice evening and report back the next morning for spy training.

After the movie, Lido and Skil listened to parenting advice from anyone and everyone who would give it. Some of the advice was serious, but most of it was stories about the kinds of questions curious Kaxian puppies might ask them, and how they might answer.

All too soon, it was time to leave.

"We know you have a long run home, so we're going to let you two escape now." Koog and Heg grinned at them.

"Bye everyone!" they said together. "Thank you for the party!"

Both their tails wagging, Lido and Skil ran off home.

As usual, Skil was the first one to turn onto their dirt road.

The sun had just started setting.

Boss and Betsy met them at the gate.

"Congratulations, you two. Welcome to the parenting club!"

Lido smiled. "We didn't expect this from you, Boss! Thanks!"

"This doesn't get you out of your patrols tonight!" Boss said with a grin.

"We didn't expect it to, Boss. Goodnight."

"Goodnight. Safe running."

Lido didn't think his belly would be coming back once he became a father. There was plenty of running to do back here at the vineyard, too. Its humans gave the vineyard pack dry places to sleep so that the Kaxians would guard the grapevines.

Of course, the humans didn't know the dogs were Kaxians.

They didn't interact with them much, either.

They were 'working dogs,' not pets.

This was Lido's forth time around the perimeter tonight. So far, all was well. He looked forward at Skil, running in front of him. All was more than well!

Wolves howled in the distance, barely audible, even to the Kaxians. Usually, Lido could understand what the wolves were saying, but not this time. The wolves must be using a code of their own, like how the Kaxians used Kanx.

Gim, one of the pack's German shepherds, caught up to Lido.

"Did you hear that?"

"The wolves?"

"Yeah. Something's going on."

Lido nodded, and they both ran to catch up with Skil.

The urge he got next was so strong, Lido only briefly looked at Skil before announcing he was leaving on an errand.

"I'm going up into the hills. A Kaxian is in trouble."

"I'm going, too," said Gim.

"You aren't going alone."

This new voice was Boss. He'd brought the whole vineyard pack with him, and five neighbor Kaxians from the vineyards nearby.

He only signaled for Skil and two others to stay home.

Ordinarily, this disregard for the patrols at the vineyard would have alarmed Lido, but tonight he thought nothing of it. He shared a loving gaze with Skil, glad she would be safe at home.

"Lead on then, Boss."

They ran out of their vineyard and up into the surrounding rocky hills. They ran for half an hour, until they each had a vision of the pack stopping to rest. They settled in a clump by the side of some large boulders, on the other side of the mountain from the Kaxian space shuttle where Skil and Lido's pack shipped their jex back to Kax. If one of them moved, it would alert all of them, they were so clumped up.

Chapter 12: Oreo

Oreo here. Yeah, I woke up real fast when this wolf bit my ear.

It was a drive-by nipping. He just ran on by, nipped my ear, and kept going.

I didn't have the chance to fight back. Not that I would've had a chance, against an entire wolf pack.

I yelped out in pain, it hurt so bad. I admit it. Then, I jumped up and looked around for more of them. Wolves always hunt in packs when they're after prey as large as I am. I smelled the one who had nipped me. I knew which way he went.

I'm not an idiot. I went the other way.

Unfortunately, that was down toward another part of town, but down sounded really good to me right then. Even toward town. Heck with these wolves. They could have their mountain! I would give up trying to live in the wilderness. I'd smelled some delicious food scents out behind some of the human dens in town. On my own, living in town wouldn't be too bad.

And anyway, I wasn't sticking around while the wolf who bit me went and got his friends.

I ran.

I ran like a scared cat!

I can run pretty fast, too.

My heart was beating faster than I ever remember it beating before. I didn't really think about where I was running, except that I wanted to get as far away from the wolves as fast as I could. There was not much chance of getting lost, though. Like I said before, these rocky hills were full of dog trails. I hadn't gone down too far before I found a trail and smelled dogs.

And then I saw something in the distance that made me sure I was crazy. Another RV sat out there on a dog trail, parked up here in the mountains, away from any human roads! It was way too wide to go on a dog trail. It had two different dog guards from those who were watching the other RV I'd seen earlier, though.

Whew! I thought maybe I wasn't crazy, after all. Maybe I wasn't imagining the RV. I mean, if it had the same two dog guards and it was way over here on this side of the mountain instead of where I had last seen it, then, yeah, that would be me imagining things. But this was clearly a different RV. Parked on a dog trail. Up away from any roads. Guarded by dogs.

Wait. Were those more dogs, pooping in front of the guard dogs? Were the guard dogs eating their poop? It sure looked like it! I'd heard of dogs who ate poop. I never understood it, but there it was, happening right in front of me. When I got over there, I planned to ask them why they did it.

What are you laughing about? That I said poop? Heh! You're funny! Poop, poop, poop, poop, poop, poop, poop, poop, poop, poop, poop, poop, poop, poop!

Anyway, I could hear wolves howling again. Lots of wolves. Way too many wolves. About eight wolves.

Did I tell you wolves hunt in packs and they are very good hunters? And one had bitten my ear?

Yeah, that wolf howling encouraged me to get my feet moving even faster, if that was even possible.

I headed down the mountain toward that RV, and here that meant going over large rocks and in between boulders. I had to watch where I was going a bit, and I couldn't see what the guards were doing.

I soon forgot about the RV for a while because I was busy being afraid of the wolf. I was sure he would show up any second with all seven of his wolf buddies. They would have a little wolf party and play a game called bite the dog. And I would be dead.

Don't get too scared.

I'm not dead.

I'm here telling you this story, so you know it worked out OK.

I heard a loud noise while I was in between the boulders. A really loud noise. I tried to explain to myself what it was, but I couldn't even think of anything it sounded like. I wondered what it was, kind of, but I was busy. Being afraid. Of the wolves.

Some of the wolves' howls had been distant, but they were all getting closer now. That biter wolf's pack was running with him down the mountain toward me. If my ears told me correctly, they would get me soon.

What was I wondering about, again?

When I got past all the boulders and down to where I'd seen the RV, I noticed something even weirder than an RV being up here away from any human roads.

Not only was that new RV not there anymore, but also, there weren't any tire tracks. The rocks it had been sitting on were charred black, as if someone had a huge campfire there. It smelled like fire, too. There were small puffs of smoke in the air, even.

Oh well.

I was pretty sure I'd seen a helicopter land and take off here earlier. Wasn't I?

Probably someone from the helicopter had a campfire. Didn't they?

Yeah, see? There was the ring of stones where many campfires had been lit, no big deal. Humans are lazy. Rather than hike up into these hills and see nature, they probably went helicopter camping up here. So they could roast marshmallows and make S'mores. Are you surprised I know about S'mores? Kids camp out in farm country where I'm from, too, you know.

I vaguely had the idea that something had been weird, but for the life of me, I couldn't remember what it was.

Anyway, I was busy. Being afraid. Of the wolves. I could hear them coming after me. They were getting closer.

My ear hurt, but there wasn't much I could do about it. I couldn't lick my own ear. There wasn't any water to dip it in or grass to rub it on, just dirt, boulders, cactus, pine trees, and sage brush.

For just an instant, I wished I was back with the new humans, where Uptight Dog would lick my ear for me. Where there was a fence around the human den, so no uppity wolf would ever bite me in the first place.

But no.

Being out here in the wilderness alone with wolves after me and getting my ear bitten was far better than sleeping in a cage and being shut up in a human's den all day and having to ask to go outside when I had to pee. It was. For sure.

I heard them close behind me then. Wolves. Not the one who had bit my ear. His scent was there with them, probably in their fur, but he had stayed behind and sent seven of his friends.

This wasn't going to be another drive-by nipping.

I would be wolf food.

I was so afraid, I peed right then and there. I'm not proud of that, but there it is.

Then the big surprise came.

From in front of me, out of the brown rocky hills came a pack of 14 dogs! They were big dogs, too: 5 Rottweilers, 4 Pitt Bulls, 4 German Shepherds, and an English bulldog. They stopped all around me in defensive poses and growled at the wolf pack.

I just kind of stood there in my puddle of pee.

What else could I do?

The wolves skidded to a stop. They raised up a little dust, they stopped so fast. Yes, these wolves were dignified and wild. OK. But they looked just as confused as I felt. I bet the wolves were thinking the same thing I was thinking:

Where on Earth did all these dogs come from?

The packs growled at each other for what seemed like ages. If the dog pack had been any smaller, there would have been a fight. It was that close. All the wolves' fangs were showing. If you think vampire fangs are scary in vampire movies, then you haven't seen wolf fangs. No, not werewolf fangs. Those are just silly. Come on. No wolf would be undignified enough to turn into a human. Get real.

In the end, the dogs beat the wolves by having

greater numbers, twice as many. There was no other reason. After a forever of dogs and wolves growling at each other, the wolves backed up the mountain.

Once the wolves had given ground, the dogs started backing down the mountain, too.

I just crouched there in my puddle of pee. I was waiting for them all to clear out and let me go on my merry way to... Well, who knows where I thought I was going. Nowhere, it turned out.

These dogs were bossy! And well informed, even far from home.

It freaked me out a little. Well, it freaked me out a lot. How did they know to come all the way up here and save me? I ask, because it was obvious that was what they had done.

These dogs were up here in the rocky hills above the unnaturally watered and green town, away from any other recent scent of dogs right when I needed them to be here in order to survive my encounter with wolves. Somehow, just like all the dogs within 100 miles of the farm I grew up on back home in strawberry country would have, these dogs knew my name and where I was supposed to be.

It was really weird.

Scary weird, even.

What made it even worse was they were all talking to each other in that slang that I couldn't understand, even howling in it and being answered by other dogs in it.

I'm telling you: that would even make you paranoid.

Another weird thing was that the English Bull Dog and one of the Rottweilers kept growling at each other. Whenever one walked past the other, they would posture for fighting and bare their teeth. Forget the threat of the wolves. I thought the two of them were going to tear each other apart. I guess they must have had a reason, but it made no sense to me!

Finally, the largest Rottweiler gave that Rottweiler a look that stopped the two of them from circling each other anymore. Then, he surprised me by speaking directly to me in a deep voice, using normal language.

"Come on, Ferd."

"What? How do you know the name they used to call me at my old humans' den?"

I tell you, this whole situation was so odd, I almost decided I had fallen asleep and dreamed the whole thing. If my ear hadn't hurt so much, I would have decided exactly that. Looking back now, I can make sense out of the next thing he said, but at the time, it went right over my head. I didn't get it.

"That's your Kaxian name, isn't it, Ferd?"

"OK, you know what? Never mind…"

I wasn't interested in speaking their Kaxian slang, even if my name fit into that somehow. I was hung up on running away and being independent, being on my own and all that. I was glad they had saved me from being eaten by the wolves, but the last thing I wanted was a bunch of other dogs telling me what to do. Humans, I can handle, but dogs are not so easily swayed by my charm. Not other male dogs, anyway.

I tried to get these dogs to leave me alone.

"…Look, I don't know who you dogs are or where you came from or how you know my old name from my old humans' den, but…"

It didn't work. Like I said before, something mega-weird was going on here.

Somehow, these dogs knew my name and where I was supposed to be, just like all the dogs within 100 miles of the farm I grew up on back home in strawberry country would have known. That was weird because these were all strangers who didn't know my mom and who lived hundreds of miles away from home.

Big Rottweiler Dude got a no-nonsense look on his face and said, "We're taking you back home to your new humans' den. Raffle and them are worried sick about you."

He must have seen how my whole body kind of deflated at that news, because he got a nicer look on his face and added, "They will be happy to see you, maybe even give you treats."

I tried looking at him sideways. "What if I don't think of it as home and don't want to go there?"

Big Rottweiler Dude wasn't impressed with my sideways look. "I guess then you'll run away again, but right now, we're taking you home."

I looked around at all their determined faces and let out a big sigh. Running around in the hills with my wolfie pals had been fun, but I supposed I had no choice but to let these dog strangers take me back to Uptight Dog's humans and their cage.

Chapter 13: Baj

Mof got to the tunnel first. He braced his paws on either side of it and blocked the others from going in, to emphasize that he was there first.

Baj bumped into his butt.

"Ouch! Watch it, Baj!

"Make me!"

"Oh, you shouldn't have said that!"

Mof unbraced his paws, turned, and bit at Baj's throat.

Baj twisted his head to the side and bit at Mof's throat.

The two of them went rolling over each other on the rocky grass.

Tef went running by, tail high and wagging.

"Whee! I'm the first one in the tunnel!"

Gat was right behind him.

"Second!"

"Third!" yelled Pim as she raced by Mof and Baj, sticking her tongue out at them.

Mof gave Baj a look that would kill if it could, and then Mof ran into the tunnel after Pim, yelling, "Forth!"

Cor, Elp, and Sah were almost there, and Baj turned around to encourage them to come faster. He wasn't letting them get ahead of him so that they would be between him and Mof. No. He just thought they needed some encouragement, was all.

"Come on, you guys! You're almost here! That's it!"

Cor stopped in front of Baj.

"Give it a rest, Baj. We saw the way Mof looked at you. You're in trouble with him again, aren't you?"

"Just get in the tunnel, Cor. Come on, Elp and Sah."

Baj followed them in.

All the puppies ran down, down, down to the end of their tunnel, which was about as long as the yard they'd just run through, 50 feet. The tunnel was just wide enough for two Chihuahua puppies to run side by side, or for one to run down toward the digging while another ran up with a mouthful of dirt, rock, or clay to spread out in the yard.

Every few minutes, their elder Nique barked a newer and weirder instruction from afar to whoever was at the top.

"The tunnel is running a bit too steep. Lessen the angle of descent by four degrees."

"The tunnel needs to turn eighty degrees to the left now."

"The tunnel is getting too narrow. Widen the forward perimeter until two of you no longer touch when side to side."

Baj had no idea how their elder Nique knew the lay of their tunnel, but their elder was a grown-up. Grown-ups knew stuff that kids didn't. Everyone knew that.

All the puppies understood these instructions. Their education in geometry had been completed before they were weaned at 4 weeks old.

They had played and bickered and made the tunnel a few feet longer by following their elder's instructions and digging this way for a few hours. And then Pim called down the tunnel.

"The small human is calling us home for dinner!"

Baj heard the small human, now that she called his attention to him.

"Come home, puppies! Your dinner is out in the yard!"

Mmmmm. Baj smelled leftover warm taco crumbs poured over their dry dog food!

Everyone else smelled them, too.

They all ran up out of the tunnel, past the shed, and through the tall grass to the gap under the wooden fence.

During his usual fight with Mof over who would go under the wooden fence first, Baj heard Mom and Dad talking about something unusual that caught his attention, even though they were speaking the harder, grown-up language and he didn't understand what it all meant.

"I told you we could shake the Kaxians up!"

"And we'll get Raffle right where we want him!"

Dad sounded aggressive. Baj hadn't seen that side of him before. How interesting.

"Yep, one of their biggest operatives."

"Won't this be hard on the kids, though?"

Mom sounded a little worried.

"Yeah, their tunnel needs to be…"

Mof was kicking Baj in the stomach, trying really hard to win the scramble to be first under the fence and over to the food.

Baj whispered in Mof's ear.

"Sh! Mom and Dad'll stop talking if they hear us!"

"So what?"

"Listen to them, Mof! It's important!"

Pinning Baj's stomach under his hind legs so that he couldn't sneak past, Mof stopped and listened.

Dad sounded confident.

"We can help them get the job done in time. It'll be alright."

"I hope so."

Mom didn't sound too sure.

Baj hoped Mom and Dad said what the tunnel needed to be done in time for, and how long he and Mof, Tef, Gat, Pim, Cor, Elp, and Sah had to get it dug. No such luck, though. They were back to talking about that Kaxian operative, Raffle.

Dad was laughing.

"I can't believe how easy his humans were to manipulate."

"Easy? This has taken a month."

"You know what I mean. You'd think a brilliant operative would have more resistant humans. A month wouldn't even come close to getting intelligent humans to leave their territory."

Mom sounded really pleased. "Well, we Niques are more intelligent than the Kaxians. You know that. So, does this mean you'll get a promotion? I think you should, Dear. You made most of this happen."

"Aw, it was a team effort, Honey. You know that. But yes, I do think I'll be moving up on this world!"

What all that meant to him and the other puppies, Baj had no idea, but he liked that his parents sounded happy and that they were being affectionate with each other.

Mof stuck his feet deeper in Baj's stomach to

remind him not to try anything, but otherwise he helped Baj block the entrance to keep Tef, Gat, Pim, Cor, Elp, and Sah from getting through and letting Mom and Dad know the kids were listening.

Gat almost ruined it. "Move out of the way if you're not going through, Mof and Baj!"

Mof stuck Baj with his feet again. "Gat, tell everyone to be quiet so that Mom and Dad don't stop talking. We're listening. You can listen too if you're quiet."

Gat turned around and sat up straight like Dad did when he told them something important. "You guys, we're listening to Mom and Dad talk. Be quiet so they don't hear you."

All of them finally settled down to listen.

Mom sounded excited now. "Ooh! I can't wait for this to all come together!"

"Well, even after they finish digging the tunnel, it won't be easy on the kids, you know, having Kaxians next door."

"Oh, that's right. I get so excited about this, and then I think of the kids again."

"We'll just have to be extra vigilant in backing them up. We're training them well. They should be able to handle it."

"I suppose we better step up the training a bit. How long do you suppose we have before Raffle's humans move in?"

"Well, that depends on Giin's operation, so we won't know until it happens."

"I'm not familiar with Giin. Is he a good operative?"

Pim poked her head in between Baj and Mof. "Can't we go in and eat now? I'm hungry!"

Baj nosed Pim's jaw. "Quiet! I want to hear how soon we're going to have Kaxian neighbors to get past when we dig the tunnel."

"Huh?"

"Haven't you been listening?"

"Not really."

"Well, be quiet and let us listen so we can tell you about it later."

"But our dinner will get eaten by rats before we get to it, we're taking so long!"

"This is real important, Pim!"

She tried to squeeze under the fence past Baj and Mof.

Baj stuck his rear paw on top of her nose, pinning her there and keeping her from talking.

She struggled to free herself, but so far Baj was keeping her quiet.

Mof let up a little on Baj's stomach. He still held it enough to tell Baj that Mof was boss, but he let up enough to show that he believed Baj now. He agreed they needed to listen, and that they needed everyone to be quiet so that Mom and Dad would keep talking. Otherwise, they wouldn't know what was going on.

Dad was going on about boring stuff, so Baj hoped they hadn't missed any good parts. "...and Giin was the one who started that."

"Alright, well maybe they'll move in sooner than later."

"Yeah, that's what I think."

Mom raised her voice and gave it a tone that let Baj know she knew the kids were up to something. "OK, kids, come on in and eat your dinner before the human comes out and takes the dishes away!"

Resuming the scramble to be the first under the fence, Baj kicked off the ground with his hind legs, banging Mof's head into the fence.

Mof cried out in pain and raked Baj's stomach with his claws.

Baj cried out in pain and bit Mof, whose head was under the fence already when he yelped in pain this time.

Mof kicked Baj in the eye and scrambled on under, yelling out, "First!"

Gat ran up behind Baj, but gestured he was letting Baj be second. "How did she know we were listening?"

Baj shrugged. "Who knows. It must be some kind of trick parents learn. Second!"

"Third!"

"Forth!"

"Fifth."

"Sixth."

"Not last!"

While the puppies ate, Mom and Dad grinned at how naive and innocent they were, and then continued their conversation.

"We're going to stop him!"

"Yep. Get him out of his little cluster of Kaxian friends there, and we will neutralize their great agent Raffle!"

Chapter 14: Lido

Skil and Lido ran together to the front gate as usual, but then they licked each other's noses and said goodbye for the day. Skil stood there and watched Lido run off toward Kaxian Headquarters for spy training. Boss and Betsy said their usual goodbyes. The rest of the dogs raised their noses to him in salute from the grape vines.

Lido looked back and saw Blackie talking to Skil. He would have to trust that Boss and Betsy wouldn't let anything happen to her. He had made her promise she would stay near Betsy while he was away during the days.

"Skil, I don't trust Blackie around you. Promise me you'll hang out with his mom all day so he doesn't dare try anything while I'm gone."

"I will. Don't worry about me. You just work on being the best spy you can be."

"I will."

Lido smiled as he ran to spy training, remembering how sweet Skil looked when she made him promise to be the best spy he could be. He ran for a few hours, made it to Kaxian Headquarters, and put his paw on the computer screen to get in. The screen showed his new job description already! How exciting!

His new boss, Eicks, was there to meet him, along with nine other Kaxians who stood behind Eicks and looked to him to do the talking.

Eicks said, "Welcome, Lido. You're the last, but that's OK. You've come the farthest. All right. Everyone, follow me!"

Eicks put his paw on a pad Lido hadn't noticed before. A door opened in the floor! A ramp went down and around out of sight. Eicks gestured with his nose for them to follow him, and he led them down into the dark.

***

Skil watched until Lido went around the bend in the road, out of sight, and then she turned to follow Betsy.

But Blackie was right behind her. Really loudly, so that his mom could hear, he said, "Why don't I go on patrol with you, Skil, now that Lido is busy with his mysterious new Kaxian duty?"

Skil had opened her mouth to tell him, "No, thank you."

But Betsy turned around and said, "Thank you, Blackie! That's a great idea. Go ahead and take Perimeter C, you two." She smiled at them and wagged her tail, waiting for the two of them to scamper off together, as if they were just puppies going out to play.

Oh no! Skil thought. What am I supposed to do? I have to obey the female alpha of our pack, even before doing what my mate and I agree on. Lido isn't going to be happy when he gets home. "OK!" was all she said to Betsy, figuring the older female didn't want to hear her whining.

Blackie smiled at her smugly. He knew Lido had

told her to stay away from him. He had manipulated her into breaking a promise to her mate.

She was furious at him.

"After you, Skil!" he said, gesturing with his nose toward Perimeter C.

***

The ramp lit up as they rounded the bend. The door swished closed behind them. At the bottom of the ramp was a huge room full of medical equipment. Two sets of clear plastic strips hung from the floor in arcs, making an air lock between the hospital and the entrance. Kaxians in white lab coats and with their noses covered in paper masks wandered around checking on Kaxians lying on padded tables.

Eicks gestured to a bin full of the paper masks.

"Put on a mask, and then we'll get you ready for your modifications for the training."

***

Still angry at Blackie for purposely making her break a promise to Lido, Skil thought to herself how she could get even with him. OK Blackie, you want to follow after me, do you? Well, I'll just see if you can keep up!

Skil took off running as fast as she could.

She knew Perimeter C. She and Lido had been running patrols around the vineyard at night, back when they went to mine with Koog's pack in the daytime.

Blackie had been running patrols at the vineyard, but he hadn't been on double duty like she had.

She left him in her dust, she was so much faster than he was.

***

Lido woke up on one of the padded tables. He

felt groggy, as if he'd slept too late and was late for mining duty. That hadn't happened since he'd gotten himself sent to the animal shelter so that Skil's humans would adopt him. The vineyard humans were much stricter than his parents' humans.

He blinked his eyes a few times, trying to get them to focus. That was weird. He couldn't make any sense out of what his eyes were showing him, but they were open, and he was pretty sure he was awake now.

"It's tricky at first."

Lido jumped off the table, the voice in his ear startled him so much. But when he sniffed to scent who was so close to him, no one was there. At least he thought no one was there. He was still having trouble focusing his eyes.

As he usually did when he was in a new situation, he raised his nose and took a big whiff. Whoa! How were so many Kaxians in here? The room was large, yes, but he smelled 500 Kaxians in here now, where he had only smelled 100 or so before he went to sleep on this padded table.

Everything was very weird.

Then he heard that voice again.

"I know it's tricky at first, but you'll get the hang of it, and then you'll be running around smelling, hearing, and seeing five times better than most Kaxians without even thinking about it."

Lido asked the owner of the voice, "Where are you? How come I don't smell you?"

The voice said, "You won't smell me. We're connected by our thoughts. You and I will always be able to talk back and forth like this. I'll help you get used to your new heightened senses. You will report to me what you find out while you're spying. I'm here on Kax."

***

Skil kept ahead of Blackie throughout the whole patrol. She stopped to drink from their water trough by the working dogs' barn often, too. She just was done drinking and off again before Blackie even got there.

At the end of their patrol, Skil parked herself next to Betsy and panted for a minute.

"I'm sorry, Dear," Betsy said.

"What do you mean, Betsy?"

"Don't worry, Dear. I won't let him chase you around anymore. I see now why he wanted to go on patrol with you." Betsy's eyebrows pushed together, and her ears went down. "We'll keep him occupied elsewhere until he gets over you. I'm sorry I didn't realize sooner how he felt."

Skil smiled at Betsy and wagged her tail. "Thank you, Betsy."

"You're welcome. Now come on! I want to show you this little storage space in the barn that I think we can fix up nicely for a puppy den!"

Wagging her tail quickly now, Skil jumped up and followed Betsy into the barn. All the working dogs slept in there all over the place, not in any assigned spots. Sure enough, there was a storage closet big enough for Skil to lie down in along with 6 or 8 puppies.

The two of them licked the area all day until it was spotless inside.

***

"My name is Saft, and I'm your voice guide, Lido. Every spy has a voice guide. All of us voice guides work here at the hall of counselors on Kax."

Lido shook himself. "I guess I better be glad to know you, Saft."

Saft laughed. "Yeah, and I better be glad to know you! And I am, Lido. Let's work on your newly enhanced senses, OK?"

"OK, good. How do I make it so I can understand what I'm seeing?"

"This is going to sound funny, but you just need to focus, Lido."

"Very funny." Lido's tail floated down to the floor.

Saft's voice was calm and soothing. "Normally, you focus your eye automatically. With your enhanced sense, it will seem automatic after a while, but for right now you need to concentrate on your eye and bring it into focus. Try focusing on your foot."

Lido looked down where he knew his foot was, but what he saw made no sense at all. It looked like a jungle of white and tan trees with no branches. An animal ran through the trees. It was all brown with long legs in back and short legs in front. It had an enormous rear end and a tiny head. It stopped and poked its head into the ground...

"Ouch!" Lido yelped and licked his foot where it hurt.

And he saw a fuzzy pink thing in front of the tan and white jungle. That was his tongue! And the jungle was his foot fur! The animal was a flea!

Lido said, "Wow, my eyesight really is enhanced."

Saft's voice said, "Yes, it really is, isn't it? Try now to see your foot how you normally do."

The jungle came back into view as Lido quit licking. He concentrated. The trees shrank. It was as if he were taking off in a flying vehicle. The trees slowly shrank and his vision rose up, up, up, until he saw his foot normally.

"Good!" Saft's voice said. "The same with your ears and your nose. You will need to concentrate for the first week or so. That is most of what your spy training will be: learning to use your new enhanced senses."

Eicks walked up to Lido then.

"How are you doing, Lido? Getting to know your voice guide?"

At being startled, Lido's eyes zoomed back in to flea vision. He couldn't see the Pitt Bull, but he did recognize his voice. He noted that smelling and hearing appeared to work as usual unless he focused on using the enhanced versions. That was good.

Lido wanted to tell Eicks he should have warned Lido this was going to happen. Lido wasn't sure if Saft could see, hear, and smell all that he could. He wasn't sure he would have accepted this job if he'd known this was going to happen. But it was done, so he had to make the best of it. That included getting along with his new boss.

"Hello, Eicks. Yeah, Saft and I are practicing the focus of my new eyes."

"Good, good. Focus on my tail now, and follow me to the training room."

"Give me a second?"

"Sure, I'll even give you 15 seconds. Go ahead, focus."

Under pressure, Lido did focus better. He had to focus first because trying to find Eicks's tail in this huge room with his eyes on zoom setting would have taken a year. He took Saft's previous suggestion and tried again to focus on his own foot. That made sense. His eyes knew right where his foot was.

He did it! There was his foot, normal looking! He looked up, found Eicks, and started following him out.

"I've got it now, Eicks. Please lead on."

"Pay attention, Lido. This room is where you will report in the morning."

They went through the clear plastic curtain, up the ramp, out the trap door, and into another door that was hidden in the entryway. This one opened using the same paw pad that opened the regular door, but Eicks bent his leg and put the backside of his paw on the pad.

"See how I did that?" Eicks said, turning to look at Lido.

Lido said, "Yes, I saw."

The training room was big and empty, except for the nine other spy recruits in it. Looking around, Lido noticed a box in the corner. It had paw pads on it, and a big red chewy looking thing.

Eicks said, "This is where you will all report every day for the next week. Let me demonstrate the kind of training you'll receive here."

Eicks went to the box in the corner and pawed the paw pad. The box made a whining noise, and then Eicks bit the red chewy thing and turned it. Light shone out of the box, and then...

Lido and the 9 other recruits were on a street in a human settlement. He could hear birds chirping in the trees and smell the freshly cut grass. A car went by on the street, and the bell rang at a school off in the distance.

Saft said, "Find the Niques with your new nose."

Chapter 15: Oreo

"Oreo!"

"Where have you been?"

"We were worried sick!"

"Come here, Puppy!"

"We're so glad you're home!"

The humans fussed over me, and you know what? I love that. I felt like I deserved some of that, so I milked it for all I could, turning over onto my back and showing them my belly. It's hard for us dogs to scratch our bellies. Our paws won't reach, and the only thing we can do is try to bend our necks sharply down so we can chew on our bellies. It kind of hurts our necks. Try it sometime.

"Oh look! He likes his belly scratched. Don't you, Oreo? Yeah."

I stretched out on my back and raised up my head to expose my neck so that she could scratch better. That made me yawn—and sneeze.

I sneezed again.

And again.

Somehow, being on my back always makes me sneeze. The female human ran into the bathroom and made lots noise with the water in there. Don't tell the other humans that being on my back makes me sneeze, or they won't come close enough to scratch my belly.

They put a new collar on me, and then, bless her heart, she noticed the sore on my ear and made a fuss about that.

"Uh! His ear is injured, Scott. Look!"

Scott came over and shined a light on my ear.

"Oh, yeah. This doesn't look good at all. C'mon, let's take him to the vet."

We all piled into the truck. The female human put me in front of her instead of in the back, and she petted my neck and back for the whole trip. I loved that.

I had no idea where we were going. I'd never been to a vet before. Turns out it's a human den where humans poke and prod us. And there are even cats there! I tried my best to chase the cats away, but the humans wouldn't let me. They held my harness and wouldn't let me leave their sides. They forgot my harness was too big, though.

Once they got themselves distracted reading magazines, I slithered out of my harness so I could go get this one cat that thought he owned the place. He was near some humans seated behind a little wall, sitting there cleaning himself like he hadn't a care in the world. I'd show him!

I charged at the cat.

The cat made a satisfying "Rrrrrreaaaaawwwlllllll!" sound and jumped clear up onto the little wall.

I would have caught him before he jumped, too, but one of the other humans grabbed the darn collar around my neck. I'd wondered what that collar was for. Now I knew for next time that I'd better get the collar off, too.

The vet brought us all into a little room and shut

the door. Darn! No more cats to chase. He put some goop on my ear and bandaged it. His area smelled just like the place inside the animal shelter where they'd given me a bunch of shots. The humans discussed those shots like they were the most important things in the world for what seemed like forever, and then finally it was time to leave that tiny room, before we all died of boredom.

I did the best I could to get that cat on my way out, but the humans wouldn't let me. They sure were against having any fun.

Once we got back to their den, they did fuss over me awhile, longer than I had expected. OK, so I went up to them and lifted their hands with my nose so that their hands were petting me. Can you blame me? I'd been through a traumatic experience!

But then as usual, the humans found other things to do. Like eating. Why couldn't they fuss over me all the time? Was that too much to ask?

Uptight Dog lay down in a corner and rested for when they told him to do something, so he could run and do it right away.

Watching the female human prepare their food wasn't all bad. I had a plan. I calculated that if I lay down in just the right place on the kitchen floor, between the fridge and the stove, then she would trip over me and spill whatever food she was carrying.

"Oreo! Up!"

Oh no, human female. I'm staying right here. I'll just pretend I don't know what in the world you're talking about. Yeah! Yeah! Just go around me for now. And then forget I'm here so my excellent plan can work. Come on! Trip over me and drop some of that beef you're carrying! It smells so yummy!

Here, maybe if I roll over while you're walking around me just so, then I can snag your foot with my leg...

But then something weird happened.

Really weird.

I saw this vision of myself getting up off the kitchen floor, and for some strange reason, I felt like I ought to do as it showed me.

So I got up.

"Oreo! Get out of the kitchen!"

"Shoo!"

The human male had come in to support his mate. How cute. Their gestures made obvious what they wanted this time.

But I'm not a trick pony.

I don't get satisfaction from pleasing the humans and causing them to call me "Good Boy." That's what makes Uptight Dog tick. He is into making the humans happy. It's called being "eager to please." That's fine. He loves his humans and they seem to love him. He enjoys making them happy. I'm happy for him.

But that isn't me. I do what I want, and it is the humans' duty to pet me when I want them to. I'm not averse to making them happy, but making humans happy is not my goal in life. I'm all about what's fun for me: hunting mostly, talking, debating, persuasion, and getting petted. And eating. Some decent treats might convince me to do some tricks.

Anyway, I wasn't planning on staying there with those humans, so it didn't matter to me what kind of treats they bought. First chance I got, I was running away again, so there was no sense in me "learning" to do as they wanted. I...

And then I saw another one of those freaky visions!

The visions were so weirdly effective at showing me what to do and making me do it. Dog! Where were those coming from? Were the humans doing that? My old humans had been different. They hadn't let us dogs into their den, so I wasn't sure if this was way different or if this was normal and my old humans were different, but something was different…

What the heck was I going on about?

I felt like going into the living room. So I did. And then I got a strange urge to chew on that stuffed dragon some more. So I did.

After the urge to chew wore off, I tried to get petted some more by putting my nose on the humans' chairs while they ate, but they didn't take too kindly to that.

"Oreo! Down!"

They pushed my nose off their chairs.

OK. Don't bother the humans while they're eating. I get it.

I followed them into the kitchen after they got up, and just so they knew I was there, I lay down right next to where they were washing dishes. I guess they had already forgotten about me, because they finally tripped over me. Too bad they were only carrying clean dishes.

Those dishes sure made a lot of noise when they crashed to the floor and broke.

This time, I high-tailed it out of the kitchen real fast.

Uptight Dog was all up in my face about that, of course.

"Why do you have to be so mean to the humans? You saw how relieved they were when you came home! They're trying to love you, and you soak it up when it suits you, but you just make trouble for them, mostly!"

I rolled my eyes. "Are you done lecturing? Because I think the nearest college is miles from here."

"This isn't a joking matter, Oreo!"

"Everything's a joking matter for me, Uptight Dog. That's why I stay happy."

"You don't seem happy to me."

"I'm happier than you are!"

He opened his mouth, but nothing came out.

Ha! I had him tongue-tied. "Dude, you're so uptight, I bet you can't go to sleep unless your bed's made."

More quiet mouth opening.

"You're so uptight, you can't enjoy anything. You're too busy playing by the rules. Doing everything the humans say. Cleaning up after yourself. You need to relax! Live a little!"

He was staring at me very intently. "I do live, Oreo, but I don't live just for fun and to please myself. I live to help others. You have no idea." His mouth opened again to say something, but he closed it. His tail went under his stomach and wagged crazy fast, like a worried puppy's.

Interesting.

"Oreo, life here on Earth is about much more than having fun. I serve a higher purpose, and that makes me happier than joking around ever could."

"What higher purpose? Doing what the humans say? Dude, they'll love you anyway. You don't have to be their little slave. You saw them love on me today, and I hardly ever do what they say." To illustrate my point and remind him of the humans scratching my belly, I rolled over on my back and wriggled around a little, using the weird cloth floor to scratch my back.

Then I realized it might look like I was exposing my weak belly to his teeth to say he was boss, so I stood up again real quick. I don't think he even noticed I was on my back, though.

He was pacing. "Obeying my humans is part of serving my higher purpose, but it is not the end, in itself. Oreo, we serve the humans so that they won't look into our activities too closely." He stood still and just stared at me.

"Wait. You do 'activities' that the humans wouldn't approve of? No way! I can't imagine that. You're making that up." I put my ears up and wagged my tail playfully.

It worked. Uptight Dog got frustrated!

He beat his front paws down. "Oreo! The humans don't know about these activities."

His ears went down, too, even his tail! Wow! I had really spun him up. How fun!

The lecture was only getting started, though. He was pacing again.

"And we don't want the humans to know what we're up to. Ironically, our bio-regeneration process makes some of us extra susceptible to bonding with humans and wanting to please them. That's what happened to me. I'm bonded to our humans, Oreo. I can't not please them."

I wanted to laugh off what he said. I meant to. I started to.

"Bio-regeneration? Ha! Ha! Ha! You should hear

yourself! A dog spouting off terms like 'bio-regeneration'!"

To emphasize just how funny Uptight Dog sounded, I rolled around on the floor, kicking my legs in the air and laughing until no sound came out. I kept it up, expecting any moment he would whine and pout at me, begging me to take him seriously. I was going to enjoy gloating over how pathetic he sounded, trying to be as sophisticated as the humans he loved so much. It was sad, really.

Finally, I got tired of rolling around and not getting a response. I stood up and looked at him.

He was standing there, grinning at me.

That was not the response that I was going for at all. It was a little creepy, if you must know.

I told him so. "Dude, you're scaring me. That is not how most dogs respond to being teased. I will give you this, though: you're freaking me out a little."

Uptight Dog's grin only got bigger.

"Think about it, Oreo: how do you, a 'dog', know what bio-regeneration means? And you do know. Don't lie. I could tell by your reaction when I said 'bio-regeneration'."

Hey, wait a second.

I did know what bio-regeneration meant.

In general, it was the process of re-growing body parts, such as when a lizard sheds its tail to escape a predator, and then the lizard grows a new tail. The fact that I knew that much was odd enough.

But I knew even more. Specifically, I knew that bio-regeneration had to do with technology that allowed the transfer of awareness from one body to another, shortly after death.

How did I know that? It wasn't anything a

hunting dog would have picked up in the normal course of his day protecting some humans' strawberry farm.

Now my own tail had gone under my belly and started wagging quickly like a worried puppy's.

Cautiously, ready to jump back at any moment if I attacked, Uptight Dog came over and nosed my jaw the way my dad might have soothed me, if I'd known my dad.

He said, "I can see I've given you food for thought. I'll let you think awhile."

I pulled myself together. He was not going to act like he was older than me when the humans weren't around! I wasn't going to let him.

"Oh, no. You don't get to act all high and mighty with me. You already admitted you're up to stuff your humans wouldn't approve of! Where do you get the idea you can act all pious about that?"

"We aren't hurting the humans, but they might be afraid if they knew what we were doing. So we serve the humans and keep their minds off things. My conscience is clear."

He sure was deeply into this delusion he had about having a secret life his humans didn't know about.

I finally pegged what about his delusion bothered me the most.

"Who is this 'we' you keep talking about? I don't see anyone here with you but me, and I am definitely not in a 'we' with you."

Without giving him a chance to answer, I ran out of the room, down the hall, over to the back door, and begged to be let out.

Chapter 16: Raffle

Constantly playing Oreo mental movies to keep him out of trouble was exhausting me. I had to get him to at least want to stay with our humans, let alone tell him he was a Kaxian!

And now he was at the back door, begging to be let out. If I didn't go with him, then he would run away again for sure.

Running to the back door to go along, I jumped over a bunch of empty boxes that hadn't been there before. I wracked my brain for things that would make Oreo want to stay with us. I had an idea: I could share my friends with him! I vowed right then that I would introduce Oreo to Lido, Heg, and the whole pack. But that would take time. I needed him to want to stay right now.

And then I had it: wouldn't Oreo love to wage war on the Nique neighbors with me?

Yeah!

A common enemy should bring the two of us closer together. Maybe I could not only make him want to stay with our humans, but also befriend him, so he would listen to me about being a Kaxian: kill two birds with one stone.

Our humans were smarter than I gave them credit for. I should have known. They came out to the backyard with us. Yeah, it was winter, but except in the mountains, a freeze is rare in Southern California. Our humans sat down on the patio furniture to keep an eye on Oreo so he couldn't dig out again.

Whew. That was a relief. I wouldn't have to be quite so vigilant. I could actually sleep sometimes. The humans being out here was OK so far as my plan went, too. They wouldn't understand anything we or the Niques said, of course.

Our Nique neighbors did not disappoint me. They came out through their doggy door and talked at us through the wooden backyard fence. They knew we couldn't get to them, so they felt free to say whatever would annoy us the most. Fred and Cherry were just as provoking as ever.

"Aw, isn't that cute?"

"Raffle and Oreo, paling around in their yard together."

"How was your little field trip, Oreo?"

"Did you get scared and run on home?"

"Oh yeah, that's right: some grown-ups brought you home!"

"If I didn't know you were three years old, I'd think you were just a puppy, too!"

Those little dogs could be so petty! I hoped Oreo wasn't too upset by them. To show him my support, I looked over at Oreo and rolled my eyes.

Still ignoring me, Oreo lifted his leg and relieved himself on a bush. And another bush. And another.

I thought to myself, *Oreo has shown me that he loves a good debate. I have to admit: he's a good debater. I bet if I engage the Niques in a lively debate, Oreo won't be able to stay out of it.*

So as not to confuse the humans, I lifted my leg

over a few bushes, too. And a few more.

The Niques had not shut up this whole time.

"Raffle cleans Oreo's ears even though he's not a puppy!"

"Ha ha! Mommy Raffle!"

I would not have to try hard at all to get mad at them. OK, I admit it: the Niques were getting to me. They had spun me up. Running over to the fence between our two back yards and yelling at the top of my lungs, I let them have it.

"At least we don't have to be in a purse to ride in the car! Or do you two have your own personal car seats?"

Gloating, I looked over at Oreo, wanting to share this special moment with him, wanting it to bring us closer and make him feel like part of our family.

No! Oreo was still ignoring me! Pretending like he didn't hear a thing, he was on his back, having our female human scratch his belly.

Our humans were a bit confused, too.

She said, "I wonder what's gotten into Raffle?"

He said, "Yeah, he usually doesn't answer those dogs next door when they bark at him.

"Maybe he's jealous that we're petting Oreo."

That did it. He called me over. "Here, Raffle!"

I ran over to my master, wagging my tail. Just hearing him call me made me happy. I met his eyes and he smiled.

He patted his knee.

I sat at his feet and put my ears back so he could pet my head. It felt nice. Like when my mom used to wash my head. Calming. My tail wagged some more. On its own, my head lifted up a little each time it anticipated his hand would pet it.

My mind was going a mile a minute, though. If the Niques couldn't get Oreo riled up, how was I ever going to get him to side with me against them? Oreo was really starting to frustrate me. How could he know a term like bio-regeneration and not be getting the rest of his Kaxian memories? Especially after that long history movie I'd fed him while he was out gazing at the stars? Why hadn't that worked?

How could Oreo or any full-grown Kaxian not know the Niques were our enemy?

Wait!

How could I not think of this before?

I didn't have to tell Oreo he was a Kaxian. I could let the Niques do that for me!

To thank my human for petting me, I washed his hand, and then I ran back over to the fence that divided the Nique neighbors' yard from our yard.

"What's the matter, Raffle?"

"Is your baby brother ignoring you?"

"Have to come talk to us because you're too lonely?"

Wow. The Niques sure had a good read on me. How were they picking up on all this? Oh well. The humans would take us inside soon, and I wanted to get the Niques to tell Oreo he was a Kaxian.

"You Niques know I'm not lonely. I have my humans, and I have a whole pack of Kaxians I can talk to. Hard working Kaxians who actually mine, unlike you Niques who only try to steal what others mine!"

There. That ought to do it. Now the Niques would confirm my story to Oreo for me!

But it was not going to be that easy.

"Aw, Raffle! You are one bored and lonely dog!"

"Making up fake friends is one of the first signs of insanity!"

"Oreo, no wonder you ignore him!"

"Yeah, stay sane!"

"We understand!"

That did it! Something inside me snapped. I hadn't even known that this something existed, but then it snapped. I was so mad, I was seeing red. I scared myself a little, with how mad I was, but I was focused on the task at hand: getting the Niques to admit to Oreo that all dogs are aliens! I lost control of my temper and started yelling at the top of my lungs at the Niques, through the fence.

"You little monsters know darn well you're Niques and we're Kaxians and you steal our jex and it's being going on for thousands of years and we try to stop you but you're so little you sneak into our mines through holes we can't block because we're so big!"

"Ha ha!"

"Raffle's lost his mind!"

"Did you hear that load of nonsense?"

"Did I ever!"

"Hey, Oreo?"

"Did you hear that?"

"How crazy is your 'big brother', anyway?"

"If you want to come live with us, just say the word, dog."

"We totally understand you don't want to live with a nut case!"

Was Oreo buying all this? What do you think? Whose argument made more sense from Oreo's point of view: my argument that all dogs are aliens from outer space, or the Niques' argument that I was crazy?

Oreo was still on his back, having our mistress pick all the dry grass and foxtails out of his belly hair, but he piped up.

"He's not my big brother, and as soon as I can, I'm getting away from him and these humans. I appreciate the sympathy and the invitation, but don't worry about me. I'm out of here already in my mind."

He said this while he was still rolling around on his back, insisting that our mistress scratch his belly. What a user!

But I was beyond anger now and into anguish. How on Earth was I going to make Oreo understand that he was a Kaxian now? I had pretty much led him into the enemy's hands, and the enemy had convinced him I was nuts.

I know what you're thinking. Why didn't I just play another mental movie for Oreo, to get him to believe me? My mental movies don't work that way. If a mind is calm, then I can suggest actions and plant visions, but getting someone to believe something is not within the power of the mental movies.

In all my 98 lives, I had never faced this challenge before: needing to remind a Kaxian that he was a Kaxian. I prided myself on meeting challenges, but this time, I wished the challenge would just go away so I could go back to mining as my Kaxian duty.

I had to do something with this anger. Looking around, I saw an old rubber chicken chew toy I hadn't played with in months. I ran to it, grabbed its throat in my mouth, and shook it as hard as I could. The physical activity helped rid me of some of the 'fight or flight' energy my body had built up when I got angry. Getting rid of that energy felt good.

Oddly, it also made Oreo jump up and run over

to me!

"Wow! Uptight Dog, you're finally doing something that isn't boring! Nice technique, too. If that were a real chicken, I think you would have killed it on the first shake. And, if it were a real chicken, I would try to steal it from you, like this!"

Oreo lunged toward me. He bit into the rubber chicken just below where I held it, and he started to shake it, too. Only, he was trying to shake it away from me.

I'm not sure why I didn't just let go. Maybe because I was shocked that Oreo was here, playing with me. Maybe because it was fun. It was!

I pulled.

He pulled the other way.

I play growled.

He play growled, too.

I shook it to try and loosen his grip.

Oreo shook it to try and loosen my grip.

I pulled and stepped over to the left.

He pulled and stepped over to the right.

I tried to back up, but he was too strong!

He planted his paws firmly in the grass and didn't budge!

And then our master called me.

"Raffle! Time to go to work, Boy!"

I dropped the rubber chicken, ran to our master, and waited for him to call Oreo, too, but nope.

Our master smiled, petting and praising me for coming when called.

"Good boy!"

I still loved hearing that! I would never get over it. I love it to this day.

Our master petted me some more, wiped my feet,

and took me into the truck by myself. Off to work we went.

For the first time, I was disappointed that I was going to work alone with my master. Don't get me wrong. I love guarding unfinished human dens with him. He talks to me through the dark night. I find out a lot about him, and I am so glad I can keep him company. Also, we work so well together, me sniffing out intruders and him telling them to get lost. I wouldn't want him to do that alone. I would be too worried he might get hurt.

But the two of us working nights while Oreo stayed home was going to make it even more difficult for me to get to know Oreo well enough for him to trust my word about our otherworldly origins, or even to make him want to remain living with us.

Ack!

Oh no!

What trouble would Oreo get into at home while I was at work?

I wasn't there to make sure he followed our female human's commands!

He would chew up her shoes! He would trip her in the kitchen! She had no idea that he was just using her and her mate for food and being petted, or that at his first opportunity, he would run away again. My humans were so trusting. I felt responsible for taking care of them. I didn't think Oreo would hurt her, but...

Now I dreaded going home, too, but at the same time I wanted to dash right on home and not even finish work. I was a nervous wreck all night.

Chapter 17: Oreo

Whew! Once we finally got rid of Uptight Dog, living with the female human wasn't half bad. Whenever she sat down, I sidled up and presented my belly, and she scratched it. She ate something that smelled delicious for dinner and didn't share it. I was mad about that until she let me lick her dish. Yes! Yum, meatloaf with mashed potatoes and gravy.

Then she put my harness on me, attached a leash, and took me out the front door. Yeah, I'm a country bumpkin, but I'm not stupid. I knew what a leash was. I hadn't ever been on one before, though. Honest!

It was a really weird feeling, being on a leash. I kept smelling things I wanted to go investigate, and she kept pulling on the leash, trying to make me not go investigate. Her idea of a walk was to go straight down the sidewalk without stopping. What use was that? Every dog knows the whole purpose of a walk is to stop and smell the pee of every other dog who has been through the area and to pee over it with your own scent. Right?

Well, no one told her.

I'm pretty strong, so I was able to investigate about half the scents that had been left on our cul-de-sac. Truth to tell, I'm stronger than she is. She was only able to pull me away by being taller and leaning into the leash. That was cheating, if you ask me.

Oh!

My attention was riveted on the squirrel that sat still at the bottom of a nearby tree, trying to be invisible by not moving. So long as I kept looking, it wouldn't dare move. I readied myself to spring on it.

I sprung! And "Ack!" The leash stopped me mid spring. My eyes jerked away from my prey for just an instant, and the squirrel dashed up the tree.

OK, going after prey is another good reason for going on a walk outside the den on a winter day. But the human had her own ideas, of course. Boring ideas.

"No, Oreo! Leave the squirrel alone. Come! We're going this way."

"This way" was on down the boring straight sidewalk that avoided all the good peeing spots. I wondered why all the humans hadn't died of boredom.

I tried as hard as I could to go to each pee spot and to chase a cat because I had to let the squirrel get away. I really tried, dragging my feet on the ground.

She tried her hardest not to let me. Most of the time, she won. Cheater.

I did get to pee on two trees kind of close to the sidewalk.

We got to the corner, and she sighed heavily then turned around, wrapping the leash around herself as she turned. Then she yelled at me, as if this was my fault.

"Ggggrrrrr! Oreo!"

I sat down, waiting for her to sort it out and get herself untangled.

She surprised me by turning back around, walking forward, and then turning to her right instead of her left, forcing me to walk in a big circle around her until we were once again headed back the way we had come.

She sure liked to do things the hard way.

Oh well.

No skin off my nose.

Next, she started barking an order at me while we walked.

"Oreo, heel!"

I wouldn't have minded, except that she yanked on the leash and yelled, "Heel" at really inconvenient times! She did it the next time a squirrel came down out of a tree, making me miss its climb back up. She yelled "Heel" when a bicyclist went by, making it impossible for me to nip at his heels, which would have been funny if it wasn't so frustrating.

Get it? She yelled "Heel," while stopping me from nipping at the bicyclist's heels!

She also yelled that out far too many times for such a short distance. We had only gotten to the first street that intersected ours. I had only tried to pee ten times. She yelled, "Heel" fourteen times as we backtracked the way we had come. She didn't give me the chance to check out anything! What a sad waste of a walk. And that was the full extent of our walk.

I really didn't understand her.

She was cranky while she was taking my leash off, too, back in the house.

"Oreo! You are the worst behaved dog I ever met! One would think you'd never been on a leash before, the way you act! Very bad boy."

I had to roll around on the floor and bend my

head this way and that while making those crying noises in the back of my throat before she finally scratched my belly.

She didn't even appreciate it when I returned the favor and licked all that goop off her face for her. I knew she didn't appreciate it because her face got all scrunched up. She didn't tell me to stop, though, and it is only polite to return a grooming favor, so I finished the job.

OK, so it was fun watching her face scrunch up like that too. I admit it.

She went with me whenever I had to go outside. I guess she wasn't as stupid as I thought.

Oh well.

I would just bide my time and wait for her or the other human to let their guard down. And then I would run away. For good this time.

I was dreading the time we would go to sleep because my last humans abandoned me in a cage, and these new humans expected us dogs to sleep in two cages on either side of their bed.

These new humans used plastic cages with smooth sides and a smooth bottom that looked more comfortable than my old cage, but the plastic cages had barred doors that could shut me in. I wasn't fooled.

Uptight Dog had told me he loved it inside because he felt safe in there. I would never understand that. All I knew was how awful it had been to be abandoned in a cage. I would have starved to death in there if I hadn't been found. I was in there for two whole days before I was rescued.

She made me get in the cage at bedtime, but she called it my house. She gestured at it.

"Oreo, go in your house."

I knew what she wanted. I'm not stupid, though. I stayed put and lay down on the carpet in front of my "house."

"Oreo, go in your house."

I kept my head down and just raised my eyes to look at her, to let her know I heard her but I didn't agree with the course of action she was suggesting.

She meant business. She picked me up and put me inside the cage! I was surprised when she stayed there near me and petted me and told me I was a good boy, didn't shut the door, and then released me from a command.

"OK!"

I bolted out of the cage and sat there licking her hand for a full minute. Her hand was the only part of her that hung down far enough from the bed that I could reach it.

"Good night, Oreo."

My fun started up again when the male human and Uptight Dog came home from work in the morning.

Of course I was at the door, ready to greet the male human when he came home. That was only polite, in case he had been injured while he was out hunting, you know. I could smell that he hadn't been hurt. I would have smelled the blood. Still, it's just what you do. Even if you are in the pack against your wishes, as a captive, as I was.

I licked at his legs a few times ceremoniously and moved in for him to pet me, since he was so tall he would have to lower himself to lick me back. I understood why he didn't lower himself. He was the alpha male of this pack. It would be unseemly for him to lower himself. I might get the idea he was below me, which he was determined not to be.

That's OK. I don't aspire to be the alpha. Too much work.

Then, just to be polite, I also licked at Uptight Dog. My tongue didn't actually touch him. I was just doing this for show, so that the alpha male didn't get angry at me for breaking ceremony.

And then his female came in and started the fun.

"Oh, look! How sweet! The puppy missed you, Raffle! Didn't you miss him, too? Let's show the puppy our love. Come on, Raffle!"

She petted me and fussed over me, to show Uptight Dog how she wanted puppies treated in her den. Uptight Dog was bonded to her and had to obey her commands! For a few fun minutes, I was glad their allied pack had returned me to them. This was just too fun to miss! She finished fussing over me and then gestured to Uptight Dog to take his turn. I couldn't resist the chance to rub it in a little, how Uptight Dog had to baby me because his human told him to.

"Yeah, lick all the wax out of my ears. Here you go. I'll make it easy for you."

He wasn't all sweetness and light, though. Uptight Dog did have the tiniest 'bad boy' side to him. He loved to torture the cat that lived in the bathroom by giving her long baths she would put up with because she really had no choice. I loved this because I figured it gave me a way to get Uptight Dog in trouble someday, with the humans.

***

The two humans tied us up outside and then proceeded to drench their truck with water and rub it down with mitts and suds it up.

I waited until they were engrossed in their task, and then I started chewing through the lead that tied me to the tree in front of the house. Soon, I would be free! No more cages for me. I would run toward the center of town this time. It had more places to hide, and it would look odd if their allied pack ran through the center of town. They wouldn't be able to track me down or return me to Uptight Dog and his humans.

I'd find a nice yard where smaller dogs lived, and move in on them, steal their food and make them hide me. I would...

Nah. I had a better vision. I would stop chewing on the lead and lie down and take a nap. Yep. That's what I decided to do. Zzzzz.

***

Uptight Dog sure hated the little dogs that lived next door. They hated him, too. He tried hard to get me to hate them as much as he did, and then they teased him in front of me for his weird pretend game about being an alien from outer space. It was funny.

We only had to deal with them when we were let outside to do our business, and that was never for long now that one of the humans always went out with me, to keep me from digging out. The little dogs were on the other side of the fence. They couldn't hurt us even if they dug under and came over here, they were so little.

I really didn't get what he was so spun up about, but I sure enjoyed spinning his wheels.

Those little dogs did, too.

"How's life with your new 'baby brother', Raffle?"

"Is it fun, babying someone two years older than you?"

Uptight Dog fell for their teasing every time! He got all bent out of shape. If they had been in the yard with us, it probably would have been bloody, but as it was, this was just funny! He roared and pawed at the thick wooden fence. As if he would actually ever damage anything his precious humans cared about. I asked him about it, and his response told me he was even more of a stooge for the humans than I thought.

"Why don't you just dig under and go end it, if those little dogs make you so mad?"

"I am bonded with our humans, Oreo. I want to please them. Digging out would upset them, let alone harming our neighbors' pets."

You see what I mean? He was really far gone. Sold out to the humans. Not even really a dog anymore, so much as a human's fur baby.

Pfft. I had no use for him, he was such a patsy. Those little dogs were way more fun, so I joined in with them and teased him, too.

"I bet the humans will be upset that we are peeing on the fence, too. Maybe you better clean that up, Big Brother."

"Very funny."

Well, he wasn't as stupid as I thought. When he walked away from our teasing and just pawed the door to tell the humans he wanted back in, I had a little more respect for him than before.

Chapter 18: Raffle

So much for the camaraderie of a common enemy. Well, I had to keep trying. My solemn Kaxian duty was to make Oreo aware he was a Kaxian. To get him to accept the fact. To make him stop teasing me! No, that wasn't why. But I sure hoped it would be a side effect.

I know what you're thinking.

You're thinking, "You have mind control. Why didn't you just make Oreo believe he was a Kaxian?"

Mind control can't make anyone believe. It can make them act as if they believe, sort of. I could make him do easy tasks as if he were serving Kax. But I would always have to be concentrating on that. Inside, he wouldn't really believe. He would still think I was nuts, the same as he had before. Only what he did would change, not what he thought on the inside, not what he believed.

Kax needed him to be himself, to think for himself, to want to help, to want to do Kaxian duty. To want to commune with Kax and to add to the conversation. Kax needed a friend, a family member, a willing helper, not a slave. Kax needed Oreo, no, needed Ferd, to believe so that our community was larger by one more mind. So that we had more company, more minds to help us mull things over.

Why didn't I just show Oreo how I could make the squirrels throw pine cones at the Niques?

Why didn't I show him how I could make the rats all come to me, or make the ants all leave their underground nests?

Surely he would have to believe me in the face of such alien abilities, right?

It would have been so much fun to use my mental movies to prove to Oreo that we are not of this world! The part of me that was just a year and a half old wanted to, kept coming up with schemes to, and daydreamed about them at work all night.

My favorite schemes always involved those two pesky Niques who lived next door. Kax! How I would love to make them look silly at the same time as proving to Oreo that we weren't all ordinary dogs related to Earth wolves. Nope, we are definitely from outer space.

In my scheme, I'd wait till my master was asleep for the day, and then I'd play a mental movie for our female human, showing her that Oreo and I could be trusted to stay outside by ourselves all day. Of course, I would tell Oreo ahead of time I was doing this, so that he could be duly impressed when it worked.

"Coincidence," I imagined Oreo would say once we were out in our backyard alone, dismissing what I'd done to make our female human let us out for the day.

I would look at him sideways and raise just one eyebrow.

"Oh, then it's just by chance she decided to trust you outside again, right after I told you I would see to it she would?"

"Yes," he would say, sitting up straight and raising

his head.

I'd be ready to challenge him with logic.

"OK, then logically, answer me this: how come you aren't thinking about digging out of the yard and running away right now, Oreo? Hm?"

He would wrinkle his brow and then get all defensive.

"I am too thinking of running away. I'm always thinking of running away."

"Well?"

"Well, what?"

"Why aren't you running away right now?"

"Because we're talking, here."

He'd do that funny nose thing where he'd try to point back and forth between the two of us, but he'd just look silly.

I would raise my one eyebrow up at him even higher.

"No. You aren't even thinking about running away. I know, because I planted a vision in your mind of you staying here in the backyard with me. You saw us sitting here talking right before we came out the back door. Admit it."

Now he'd be looking at me sideways. "Go on."

"Oreo, we're both aliens, you and me. We come from outer space. All the creatures you call 'dogs' do. We big Kaxians come from Planet Kax. The smaller Niques come from Planet Nique. We're here on Earth to mine jex. We are not of this world, and some of us, born to lead, have otherworldly abilities. Do you follow me so far?"

Oreo's teeth show in a tight smile. "You better get this all out before I bolt."

I smile my nicest smile back, trying to show I

want to be his friend. "Showing you the movie of our mistress letting you out just before she did, well, that was a demonstration of my elite alien powers, part one. For part two, I'm going to involve the enemy: our neighbors next door, the small dogs."

"Yeah, I know you don't like them. But C'mon. 'The enemy'? Isn't that language a little strong?"

Oreo's bravado is good, but his tail is under his belly.

I'm making an impression, so I rush on into my explanation.

"You have no idea. That language isn't even strong enough to convey how bad the Niques are. We Kaxians were here on Earth first, and yet the Niques do all they can to steal the jex we Kaxians mine, including play mind games. They are manipulators."

Oreo laughs, but his tail is still under his belly.

"Whew. You sure are laying it on thick!"

He is inching toward the outer fence, no doubt indeed finally having thoughts of digging out and running away as fast as he can. He doesn't believe me yet, but he knows something is not as he thought it was.

I get between him and the outer fence and keep talking.

"Yeah, well. All dogs are aliens. We are not the same kind of aliens as the little dogs. That's why they're always giving us grief."

He bristles all his fur so he looks bigger than me, but his tail is still under his belly.

"Why can't you just be happy being a dog? Why do you have to be a special alien? I like being a dog. Why can't you?"

He is inching around me to get toward the outer

fence.

I block him and gesture with my nose toward the other fence, the one between us and the Nique neighbors.

"Come with me and look through the fence. I want you to see this."

He gets this tone in his voice like he's humoring the crazy one until he can escape.

"Oh. K."

On stiff legs, he follows me over to the Niques' fence.

We both put our eyes right up against the cracks between boards in the fence, so we can see into the Niques' backyard. His tail is still under his belly, wiggling like a little puppy's. It's sort of cute, but I feel bad for him. He's such a manly Kaxian that he would be extra embarrassed if he knew I knew he was scared.

I pretend not to notice.

Looking him straight in the eye and raising my eyebrow again, I point with my nose at the Nique neighbors' door.

"If I were just an ordinary dog and not an alien, would I be able to make the little neighbor dogs do this?"

I make sure he's looking.

He is.

Exactly two steps apart like they were in the synchronized swimming event in the Olympics, both our little Nique neighbors run out their doggy door. Switching to a high trot that brings their paws up to their eyes, they circle around their doghouse three times. Pausing, they both rear up on their hind legs and twirl around three times, then came back down onto all fours, bending their front legs in a bit of a bow. Finally, they both run back in through their doggy door.

Oreo's tail has come out, and he's wagging it in glee, with a big grin on his face.

"You made them do that?"

Now he's laughing, shaking his whole body, completely relaxed.

"Yeah."

I perk up my ears and sit up straight, proud.

His tail wags like he's having the best time ever.

"Make them do something else!"

My ears go down and then back up. "Like what?"

Oreo's nose goes up and sniffs three times.

"Mmmmmm! It's just about lunch time, don't you think? Make them steal some of that delicious-smelling beef their female human is preparing, and make them come give it to us through that knot-hole in the fence!"

I grin at him.

"No problem."

A few minutes later, we're chowing down on some tasty beef.

The Niques are quiet and probably confused on their side of the fence for a few minutes, and then they get back to insulting us, like they've forgotten anything weird happened.

"What's going on, Raffle?"

"Are you locked out of your humans' den?"

"Too bad you don't have a doggy door so you can go in whenever you want!"

"Yeah, you poor dogs have to beg to be let in or out!"

"I would hate that!"

"Yeah, I bet you hate that."

"I sure would hate to be you!"

I raise my eyebrow at Oreo, asking if he is yet convinced that the Niques are the enemy.

He paws the dirt like he's ready to go over and fight them, so I show him my favorite tricks to play on the Niques.

"Watch the squirrels," I tell Oreo, pointing with my nose up into the pine trees on their side of the wooden fence.

The squirrels all grab pine cones in their tiny little hands. They throw them at the Niques, who shout out in pain and run in through their doggy door.

While we wait for the Niques to come back out, I make the squirrels do tricks in the trees.

The squirrels do flips. They leap from one tree to the next, sort of like they're flying. They carry bunches of pine cones while walking on skinny branches. Squirrels are really good at doing tricks.

Finally, the Niques came back outside to mouth off at us some more.

"Are the two of you still outside?"

"Aren't you getting hungry?"

Oreo and I both laugh at this.

The Niques don't remember bringing us food, so they just bluster through it.

"Aw, nervous, huh."

"Your humans will let you in eventually."

"Yeah, they have to, right?"

"They do love you, don't they?"

"Of course they do."

Oreo surprises me and opens his mouth to say something in defense of our humans, but I shake my head at him.

"Pigeons," I say to Oreo, pointing my nose up into the sky.

The pigeons all take aim and poop right on the Nique neighbors' noses. The Niques whine and run back into their doggy door again.

We roll all over the yard, laughing our hardest!

Together in my imagination, Oreo and I scheme up all kinds of ways to get back at the Niques for being so obnoxious. Making them dig out and then scratch on their front door, so they'll get in trouble with their humans. Making them dig over here into our yard and give us both baths, but ew! No! Making them let a skunk into their humans' den. We have them make funny faces. Dance crazy dances. And say nice things about us when their Nique friends are over.

And then of course Oreo knows and believes that all of us big dogs are Kaxians. He remembers his previous Kaxian lives and is happy to do his Kaxian duty and understands that part of that is making his humans happy so they won't suspect anything.

Yeah, that's how it happens in my daydreams.

I wish I could have just done that.

But I couldn't.

Showing off would have been a far easier way to do my Kaxian duty. However, the part of me that remembered 98 other lives here on Earth with all the lessons learned reined me in every time I was tempted to show off. All it had to do was remind me that I had to protect our Kaxian presence on Earth. I couldn't let my showing off clue the humans in to my alien abilities. I had to uphold the primary edict from Kax:

No humans can know that dogs are aliens.

I couldn't risk telling Oreo about my special abilities or letting him realize I had them. At the very least not until there was basic trust between us. So far, there was anything but. As our relationship currently stood, my new 'brother' would do everything he could to sabotage anything he perceived was important to me.

No, he wasn't going to listen to me unless we had a common bond. Whatever I said to him about anything important was just going in one ear and out the other.

Still, Oreo had to be lonely.

Maybe if I brought some of the pack around to meet him and make friends, then he would open up and want to be part of what we all had together.

Yeah, that's what I would do.

At night while I was at work guarding empty new human dens with our male human, I barked out a relay in Kanx to let Heg know my plan.

"Heg, Ferd needs some Kaxian friends."

I heard my message relayed a few times, and then Heg's answer was relayed back to me.

"Raffle, does Ferd really not know he's a Kaxian? Still?"

I could hear a bunch of side discussions starting about that. I kept at our main discussion.

"Heg, correct, Ferd does not know he's a Kaxian. Can you get Lido to visit us?"

My human noticed how much I was talking and took an interest.

"Raffle! What you so excited about, Boy?"

He put down the huge flashlight he wielded like a weapon, went down on one knee, and beckoned to me.

I felt terrible for making my human think anything was wrong. I rushed over to him and nuzzled his hand.

He petted me and hugged me.

I sat there with my ears folded back for a few minutes so that he would keep petting me. It was calming him, too. I could sense that.

It took longer than usual, which made me nervous despite being petted, but Heg came through. I heard the relay, loud and clear.

"Raffle, yeah, it's arranged. Lido will come visit you tomorrow. Good idea. We all agree that Ferd needs Kaxian friends."

Chapter 19: Oreo

Uptight Dog was crazy. He worked nights, but instead of sleeping during the day like a normal dog, he stayed up and chatted with his buddies all day. One by one, they would come by the house. We couldn't go outside unless the female human took us, so he and his buddies would chat through the window.

If he put his front paws up on the front living room window, then he could see our visitor and be seen. It was a little loud, chatting through a window, but the female human's office was in a bedroom down the hall. She was on the phone all day and didn't notice what he was doing. It had to look funny to the neighbors, though, all these dogs coming by to stare through the front window and bark at the house.

The dog who came by most often was one of those who had saved me from the wolves a month ago, the Bulldog named Lido.

"Hey Raffle!"

For some dumb reason, Uptight Dog always turned to me and smiled when a dog came to the window, like I would be just as happy to see his old buddy as he was. As if I was included or something. Please.

"Hey Lido! How are Skil and the pups?"

"We're all doing great! The pups are almost

weaned."

"Already? It seems like they were just born yesterday!"

"I know! Bip opened his eyes after just nine days, too."

"Wow!"

"I know. He's one to watch, I'm telling ya."

Those two were obviously best friends. They had lots to talk about. I only had being rescued in common with the Bulldog, and I wasn't going to bring that up any time soon. Too sissy.

Besides, the Bulldog was weird.

No, I mean it.

He was weird even besides wanting to be friends with Uptight Dog. His gaze would drift while he was talking. Instead of looking you in the eye, he'd be staring into space.

No! I didn't talk to him, but I watched while the two of them talked. It was creepy, the way his eyes wouldn't be focused on Uptight Dog, but just staring off into space. It was like Lido was a zombie or something.

And then there were the days this dude Heg would come over. Uptight Dog talked with most of his friends, but with Heg, for the first minute or so the two of them just sat there, smiling and watching the birds fly around or something.

And then of course Heg would talk to me as if we were best buds just like him and Uptight Dog. It made me uncomfortable.

I wanted to say to Heg, "Dude, I just met you. I don't want to hear about all your personal plans and stuff. Let's play some tug o' war or run around and sniff trees together until we have something in common before we go talking about personal stuff," but that would have gotten me talking to him. I just kept my mouth shut. Yeah! I did.

Don't you hate it when someone acts like you're best friends when you barely know them? It made me wish we had a doggy door more so I could get away from Uptight Dog's friends than so I could escape from the humans!

Uptight Dog was also nuts about the humans. He really loved them, and wanted me to as well. He just didn't get that the last humans I'd trusted had left me in a cage to die of starvation, so I wasn't ever going to trust any humans. Never again.

The only uses I had for humans were to get food and to get my belly scratched.

They kept trying to get me to sleep in the cage they called my house.

She was pretty good about scratching my belly whenever I rolled over onto my back.

I kept telling the male human he should take me to work, too, but the female human would hug me and tell me my duty was to stay home and protect her.

"You're *my* puppy. Yes you are. Raffle is Scott's dog, but you're *mine*."

I'd been with these humans a month when they started bringing boxes home. They brought home big boxes, little boxes, and medium size boxes, dozens of them, maybe hundreds. A few of the boxes were plain and brown, but most had pictures on them and smelled like food, cloth, plastic, metal, or other human things. I didn't get too interested until they started putting their own human things into the boxes, especially when they put food in the boxes.

Were they storing up for winter? Did these

humans hibernate? Who would feed me if they hibernated? Oh no! Would they expect me to hibernate in the cage?

I got so panicky I actually went on my own to talk to Uptight Dog. Just to see what was up. This didn't mean we were friends or anything. Never that.

"How long have you been with these humans?"

"I've been with these humans for more than a year."

"Do they hibernate in the winter?"

"No! Why would you think that?"

"Why are they piling up all these boxes?"

"Oh! They're getting ready to move."

"Move?"

"Yeah. They've done it before. They pack up all their stuff and move it to a new den."

"Oh. I guess their hunting has dried up here?"

"Something like that."

"So you're sure they don't hibernate?"

"Heh, yeah I'm sure."

Well, that was a load off my mind. It was bad enough being abandoned in the cage. Imagine slowly starving to death in a house full of food while your humans slept the winter away!

It took forever for them to pack all those boxes. A month anyway.

Lido kept coming by and staring into space while telling us all about his and Skil's litter of puppies.

Heg kept acting like me and him were best buddies and wanting me to join the two of them when they talked.

I kept leaving whatever room they came into. I finally had to pretend to be asleep before they quit trying to get me to join in their boring conversations.

The female human kept trying to get me to heel when I was on the leash.

And, Uptight Dog kept trying to get me to fight the neighbor dogs next door.

Finally, all the boxes were packed and loaded up onto a big moving truck that towed the human's little Nissan truck. Now, all I had to worry about was what kind of den we were gonna move into.

Oh, and how I could escape while we moved.

I saw my chance when we were all in the big moving truck and we stopped for gas. The male human was pumping gas, and the female human went inside the store. The door to the truck didn't close all the way.

I had a secret: I could wriggle out of my muzzle and harness whenever I wanted to. They were both too big.

I started to wriggle. The hardest part was getting my elbows through. I had one front leg through and was wriggling down to bring my other front leg through when I noticed a squirrel on the sidewalk a block away.

I had to keep my eye on that squirrel or it would get away! I was really good at that. I stood absolutely still and didn't even move my eyelids. I would show that squirrel who was boss. It wasn't going to get away on my watch!

I was still watching the squirrel when the male human came back to the truck.

"Do you need to go potty, Oreo?"

"Not right now. I'm busy watching that squirrel."

Of course, humans don't understand dog speech. He totally misunderstood.

"OK, let's get you out of the truck so you can...

Ahhhhh!"

His mate was back with a bunch of wonderful smelling food from the store.

"What's wrong?"

"Oreo got halfway out of his harness and all the way out of his muzzle!"

"No way!"

"Yep, way. Oreo! You are getting small sized muzzle and harness to wear from now on, first chance we get!"

"For now, I guess we can't leave him alone in the truck."

"Right, one of us will always have to stay with the dogs until we get him a properly fitted muzzle and harness."

They both sighed and then smiled at us and petted us. They were sickeningly sweet. So much for my big secret. Oh well. I would just bide my time. There was bound to be another chance to escape.

Uptight dog was in for a big surprise, though.

He expected us to drive the moving van a few miles down the freeway at most, hopefully toward his friends Lido and Skil. But we went the other way. And we kept on driving, and driving, and driving. We moved a lot farther away than he was ready for.

I could see the loss playing out in his eyes, he wore his emotions so plainly. Lido wouldn't be visiting us anymore. No one from the old neighborhood would.

Not counting the time we stopped for food, it took about 3 hours to drive to the new den, at 70 miles per hour. It would take all day to run there from his pack's territory, and I couldn't see anyone with puppies of their own being gone a whole day. I couldn't see much of anyone at all taking off for a whole day to go visit a dog who didn't live nearby anymore.

The moment Uptight Dog realized we were leaving his pack's territory, he scared his humans by barking and howling up a storm. The female turned around in her seat to make sure he hadn't been injured, and the male pulled over to also make sure. They got out of the moving van and opened the door and examined him. Of course, they didn't find anything wrong.

The male human got back in the driver's seat and started up the truck. The female turned in her seat and petted and comforted her dog.

For a full ten minutes, Uptight Dog just kept howling and barking as if his poor heart would break. It was in that weird slang everyone in his territory used, so I couldn't understand it, but I could imagine what he was saying. I could hear what he said being relayed, and answers being relayed back. This is what I imagine they said:

"To Heg from Raffle: My humans are moving me far away! This might be the last time you hear from me! I love you! I will miss you forever!"

"To Raffle from Heg: You're a good pack-mate and friend. You will be missed. We love you, too."

"To Lido from Raffle: Take good care of the pups! I'll miss you, Buddy! Sorry I can't stay to see them grow up. My love to Skil!"

"To Raffle from Lido: Take care, Buddy! We'll miss you! We love you!"

"To Lido from Raffle: But I love my humans more! You know I must stay with them. I promised to. I'm a goody goody dog who always does what he's told!"

Yeah, I know he probably wasn't saying that last part, but I think he should have been made to hear how pathetic he sounded. He even made me feel sorry for him. Just a little.

Uptight dog took the move pretty hard. For the rest of the drive, unless the humans were paying attention to him, his normally perked ears were always back against his head, and his tail lay still and didn't wag.

Chapter 20: Lido

Lido raised his nose up toward the full moon in the middle of the vineyard and howled in sorrow.

Skil ran to him and howled alongside her mate for the departure of their mutual friend.

When they had howled away their sadness, they looked at each other. At the same time, both of their eyes moved toward where their puppies nested in the barn. They smiled at each other, turned, and ran to their family.

Bip, Kip, Fip, and Glip were all still in the barn, but Bip had one foot outside.

"Bip! I told you to stay in the barn!"

"But Mom! All the excitement is out here. You and Dad are howling!"

"It's not excitement, Bip. We're going to miss our friend Raffle."

"Well, it's more exciting than anything else that happens around here."

Lido laughed. "You'll see excitement soon enough. OK, time for bed."

***

The next morning, Skil saw Lido off to work, and Boss and Betsy waved to him from the front gate. Blackie was off on patrol, far away.

Saft's voice said, "Right. Let's go back where we saw that speedy Nique yesterday. I bet today's the day we figure out their speed."

"I hope so."

Lido ran to a human neighborhood near another Kaxian pack's mining site. When he got within the outer patrol perimeter of the mine, he barked out in Kanx so they wouldn't worry about what he wanted.

"Lido here on auxiliary patrol."

A few relays later, there was a reply.

"Welcome, Lido. Let us know if you need anything."

He found a place to hide, and then he tuned his nose up to its higher capabilities. Wow. This was always a rush. Thousands of scents came to him, and each one brought the idea of where it came from. It took him a good half hour just to take it all in.

And then he knew exactly where all the Niques in this neighborhood were.

Saft's voice said, "Good. Let's move in on the Niques at 4 o'clock."

Lido ran three miles in that direction, up a steep hill, and chose another hiding place in some bushes, where he hunkered down. It was a great vantage point. He was looking off the top of a cliff down onto the neighborhood. He wondered just how much Saft knew about his surroundings. Had Saft known he would be looking down off this cliff? How?

Saft's voice said, "Perfect. Now sniff out one of those Niques that is moving extra fast and then focus your eyes in on it so we can see what makes it run so fast."

Something told Lido that the 'we' Saft spoke of meant more than just Saft and Lido. He knew then that it meant everyone in the Counselors' Department back on Kax. He knew that whatever he saw, heard, and smelled was being transmitted back to Kax somehow.

Dutifully, Lido sniffed the air, opening his nose up to its new capabilities so that all the scents for miles around came to him. They almost overwhelmed him, they were so much more than he was used to. There. The closest Nique moving extra fast was right there.

"Well done," Saft's voice said. "Now allow your nose to guide the focus of your eyes, and we should see that Nique in action, whatever it's doing."

Lido concentrated on the scent of the nearest Nique and willed his eyes to focus in on it. There it was!

***

Leba the female Volpino was late meeting up with her pack. She was only supposed to use her extra speed for pack business, but catching up with them was business, right? She dug out of her humans' yard, scratched to pour on the speed, and whoosh! She was off running!

She caught up with her girlfriend Tica the toy poodle and turned off the speed just before they got to the pack's meeting point. She and Tica were the only two females in their pack, so they hung out together.

Tica said, "Oh! My, Leba, you nearly gave me a heart attack! You're so fast! Hee hee!" Tica's laugh was really cute.

Leba said, "Sorry, Tica. I didn't mean to scare you. I just didn't want to be late!"

Tica said, "Oh, I know. Rufe can be truly rude when he sets his mind to it. Don't you think?"

Rufe was their pack leader. He was a Scottish Terrier. The other males in the Nique raiding pack were Yoga and Ceep the Pugs, Lad and Pad the Shetland Sheepdogs, Mesky the Cockerpoo, and Zeit the Border Terrier. OK, there was one other female in the pack, Woogies the Cockerpoo, but Leba and Tica didn't associate with her. Their mothers had told them not to because she was too rude. Sort of like their leader.

Rufe the pack leader said, "Very well, if we're all here, then let's start." He sat down and waited for everyone to sit down in neat little rows, be quiet, and listen to him, and then he continued. "The farmers market trap is working really well, so today we will see if we can lead some more Kaxian recruits there. If you understand the plan, then say, 'Yes, Rufe.'"

They all said, "Yes, Rufe."

Rufe said, "Very well. Let's go find some Kaxians to lead into the trap. Two lines, everyone. Run in formation. Let's go."

Leba and Tica stuck together as usual, following after all the guys, and Woogies.

Tica said, "So, do you like my new manicure?" She pranced a little extra fancily as she ran, so Leba could see her nails.

"Very nice! Ooh! I love that color on you!"

Tica stopped for a second and scratched her head with her hind leg.

"See how nice it looks when I comb my hair?"

"How pretty! It really brings out your eyes!"

They both started running again, faster, to catch up with the guys.

Tica said, "You think so?"

"Oh yeah, very much so. They did a good job. Did you go to that place behind the new grocery store?"

"No, we went to that new place inside the new mega store."

Leba said, "We can go in there?"

"Yes! So long as we stay in the cart!"

All the guys stopped then, so Tica and Leba stopped a few feet behind them. 'Close enough to hear, but not too close,' as the two of them put it. They didn't like any of the guys, and they only showed up to pack duty days because their parents made them. Shopping and lunching with their female humans was much more fun.

Yoga the Pug stared at them and slobbered as usual, but they ignored him.

Rufe said, "Very well, here come some Kaxians.

Make a show of playing until they notice us."

All the guys started playing this stupid game of 'jump the highest' that they always played. Woogies ran round and round them, shouting insults. She was kind of confused, if you asked Leba and Tica. The two of them each played a more dainty game of 'catch my tail'. Of course, they didn't go too fast. They had learned that wasn't ladylike.

Rufe said, "Right. They've noticed us. Now go lure them off to the trap, Leba, Tica, and Yoga.

Leba and Tica both opened their mouths to complain about being sent off alone with Yoga the Pug, but Rufe cut them off, saying, "No arguing! Now get moving!"

Tica and Yoga ran toward the Kaxians at normal speed, calling out the normal insults that always caught young Kaxians off guard and made them easy prey when it came to luring them into traps.

"Did you miss the doggy day care bus?"

"Aw, out in the big bad world without your Mommy?"

It was Leba's job to be the fast Nique the Kaxians couldn't catch. She would keep insulting the Kaxians long after the others quit, so that they tried to catch her and ran all the way into the trap. Again, Leba scratched to pour on the super Nique speed, and whoosh! She was off running faster than Niquely possible!

She didn't know she was being watched by the intelligence agency of an entire planet.

Chapter 21: Oreo

The humans were all excited about moving into their new den. They called it 'our first house' in tones that made even me a little curious to see it. They made the new den sound so special.

They wanted their favorite dog to share in the excitement. He tried, but I could tell he already missed his good friend Lido and the rest of their pack. Unless his beloved humans were paying attention to him, he moped around with his ears and tail down.

I don't know why, but I felt like I should do something to make him feel better. I felt sort of obligated to him in some stupid way. I knew that was all nonsense, that emotion stuff. Following your emotions only gets you hurt. Silly me for feeling like I should be nice to him just because his emotions had gotten him hurt. What was I thinking? I didn't want to wind up like him.

The humans were really enthusiastic.

"Raffle! Come see your huge new back yard!"

"Oreo! Come, too!"

They had just pulled the moving truck up into the horseshoe driveway of their new den. We were still in the sage brush desert, but we'd climbed uphill and were now about 2,000 feet above the sea. The air was thinner up here. My nose told me the ground had recently been frozen, and snow had fallen here. The houses in this new neighborhood sat back from the street. There could have been ten times as many houses, but they were spread far apart.

By city standards, our new territory was huge. The humans called it half an acre. Of course by country standards it wasn't very big at all, not even big enough to grow grapes correctly, if what I'd heard from my previous humans was any indication. Still, I caught myself thinking we dogs could be happy here. There was enough territory to stretch our legs and even hunt a little.

The humans unbuckled us from our seat belts, snapped leashes onto our harnesses, petted us way more than my other humans had my whole life before, and walked us to the side of the house where we went through a gate into the back yard.

"Here, Boy! Get the ball!"

The male human threw a tennis ball across the yard. How random and strange.

Uptight Dog dutifully went and fetched the ball and brought it back to him. I was thinking what a patsy that dog was. He actually seemed happy to be running and getting a ball for his human, though. Only a few minutes ago even his tail had been still, being sad about moving so far away from his friends.

"Good boy, Raffle! Get it, Oreo!"

I like fun just as much as the next dog.

I do.

But running after a ball is not my idea of fun. I let the humans know that by lying down with my head on the ground and raising only my eyes to look up at them. I hoped the message was clear: they could not expect me to play such a silly game. I was too mature for such things.

For the moment, I kind of forgot I had them convinced I was a puppy.

Uptight Dog could barely contain himself, his whole body shaking with the urge to chase after it for them. He was so eager to please them and for them to have fun. He played by the rules, though. They had called that ball for me, so he just sat there twitching. All it would take was a look of encouragement from one of the humans, and he'd be after that ball.

"OK Raffle! Go get it!"

He tore off so fast you would think the house was falling down on him. The good thing about it was he kept them entertained for a while, so I had time to explore my new territory as a dog should.

At first glance, the yard was just dirt and trees. The trees were large: four ash and three pines. I found burrows for snakes and gophers, and the droppings of many types of birds, some of which sang in the huge trees, even in winter. I smelled squirrels, too.

I also found a strange burrow that smelled like Chihuahua dogs. It was a recent burrow, still in use. The strange thing was, the yard it was under smelled like horses and Rottweilers. The Chihuahuas lived on the other side of us.

Here, let me explain what was where.

Our new backyard was separated from most of our neighbors by chain link fences.

The only wood fence was between us and the yard to the right as I entered our backyard from the street. That one smelled like Chihuahua dogs, and sure enough I could hear them yipping inside their house, eight puppies and their parents.

The yard to the left of us smelled like horses and Rottweilers, but the horses hadn't been there in a long time. The scent of two Rottweilers was more recent, but I didn't hear them right now.

The street was to the south, on the other side of our house.

North of us, across a small dirt alley, I could see three more chain link fenced yards.

A beautiful German Shepherd mom and her four pups were in the center yard pretty much all the time. I don't think the humans let them inside their den. The mom was a rare cream-colored and blue-eyed German Shepherd. I said hello to her every chance I got.

The yard to my right of the German Shepherd mom's was empty.

Two aggressive dogs were in the yard across the alley on the left, a Bull Mastiff and a Pit Bull. From hearing their humans talk to them, I knew their names were Roy and Ocho. They were snarling at us across the dirt alley through the corner of their chain link fence.

"Don't you dare come over here!"

"You do, and you're dead meat!"

"We'll eat you!"

The slammed their bodies against the fence to demonstrate how strong they were and how much they meant their threats.

They didn't need to worry. I had no interest at all in trying to go into their yard. But I tried to act cool with these tough dogs.

"That's OK. We're doing just fine over here! Thanks for thinking of us!"

But all I got was disrespect for my trouble, from the humans.

"Oreo! Be quiet!"

I had drawn the attention of Uptight Dog's humans away from their stupid game of 'Get the ball.' I was mad at them for disrespecting my attempt to establish proper neighborly relations with our rude new neighbors. I stood up straight and told them so, trying my best to explain the situation.

"Wait a minute! You shouldn't be telling me to be quiet! I'm defending you! I'm guarding the back entrance to your den! Those guys over there are talking trash to all of us. I need to tell them we aren't going to put up with that, right here and now, or it's going to be nothing but trouble from them from now on. You better not be telling me I'm in trouble for defending all of us!"

I was so caught up in my role as a defender that I'd forgotten the humans couldn't understand me. Of course they couldn't understand me.

"Oreo! Quiet!" the humans yelled again.

That made me so mad that I gave up on trying to defend Uptight Dog's new yard from his new neighbors. It made me remember that I was so out of there. What was I even bothering with this? First chance I got, I was going to dig out and run away again. I told myself, "Who needs this territory, anyway? Not me."

But then I sensed trouble, and my guarding instincts kicked in again.

Uptight Dog was back by the new neighbors, looking for the ball his human had thrown. It had gone down a little hole, so he was having to dig to get to it. He's so obedient, and they'd told him to get the ball, so he was going to be there digging until he got to it.

The hard-packed desert soil is full of rocks and clay, so he was having a difficult time of it.

And sure enough, as soon as Uptight Dog had gone back into that corner near Roy and Ocho, they had laid into him for being too close to their territory. I had tried to tell the humans those two would be trouble. They were laying it on extra thick.

"Get away from our end of your yard!" Roy said, slamming into the fence for emphasis.

"Yeah, that end of your yard is our territory," Ocho said with another slam into the fence.

Uptight Dog was doing his best to mind his own business and get his human's ball out of that hole so he could go back to him. I could tell he was afraid, though. He cringed every time Roy or Ocho slammed into the fence.

Even though a dirt alley and two chain link fences separated our two yards and they couldn't actually attack us, their threats were having the desired effect on him.

That made me mad!

I started so fast when I ran over there that I tore off chunks of the packed desert soil with my claws. And then I gave those bullies another piece of my mind.

"Our yard is not your territory! Hear that? It's OUR yard. You can yell at us until your tongues hang out of your mouths, but we will do just as we please in OUR yard!"

I was getting into it, too. My fur was all bristled out so that I looked as big as I possibly could. I was right up there in the very corner of our yard, as close to Roy and Ocho as I could get. I didn't slam myself into our fence, though. I wasn't trying to threaten them, just telling them to quit threatening us.

Roy bristled himself up big and puffy, as if he needed to, and tried to make me back down.

"You better watch yourself. We might dig out of here and dig in there to come get you."

Ocho bristled himself up big, too, but I could hardly tell because his fur was so short. He joined in on trying to make us cower before the two of them.

"Yeah, you wouldn't be standing up to us if we were in there with you!"

Uptight Dog looked at me and shook his head. His eyebrows were all pinched together, and his tail was jiggling under his belly. He was still frantically trying to 'get the ball' for his human.

His fear only made me more determined to get Roy and Ocho to leave him alone. It was like his need for a defender triggered my instinct to defend him, even though he was giving me that look, trying to get me to just drop it.

I wasn't going to drop it.

"What do you think I am, a city dog like you? Nope, where I'm from, not even tiny dogs like those next door let anyone claim their territory. This is our territory now. Our humans claimed it, and we're defending it."

Our humans came over and grabbed our harnesses to pull us away from the fence, away from the vicious looking dogs who were barking so loudly.

"Good boy, Raffle. Never mind that ball. We'll get you another one."

The male human led Uptight Dog into the house.

The female human attached a leash to my harness and petted my head in a soothing way.

"Come on into the house, Oreo."

I kept myself between her and our harsh new neighbors all the way to the house, and I watched them so that I would know if they carried out their threat to dig into our territory.

Chapter 22: Raffle

Most veterinarians have separate entrances for dogs and cats, and that's good. But I haven't yet seen one smart enough to keep separate entrances and waiting areas for big dogs and little dogs, that is, Kaxians and Niques.

Moving so far to a new den was lousy in more ways than one. Not only did it mean the pack was out of anything but extra-long range or Kax communication, but it also meant that Oreo and I had to meet with a new veterinarian. I loved the parking lot. It had all these little ceramic cacti to pee on! The building looked like a Spanish mission, in keeping with the desert theme. The waiting room was large, with lots of wooden benches.

Five dogs were waiting ahead of us, with their humans. I greeted the four Kaxians, but the one Nique, a little Weiner dog, was giving us all a headache with his high-pitched bickering.

"Get out of my vet's office, all you big lugs!"

He kept running under his male human's legs, and then out again to yell at us.

"You're not welcome here!" Under the legs.

"This is my territory!" Peeking out.

"Cause I said so!" Back under the legs quick, like a turtle.

"You're all trespassing!" Just his nose peeking out.

"If I wasn't on this leash, I would make you leave!" Chasing after one of us Kaxians as he was leaving, anyway.

"And don't you forget it!" As the door closed and the Kaxian left with his humans.

Aren't Niques hilarious? The way they always provoke us Kaxians, I mean. I was disturbed, though. Not once had this Nique referred to us all being aliens. No digs at Kax. No boasts about Nique. This could only mean one thing: he was in on the Niques' effort to keep Oreo in the dark about being from Kax.

At the same time, the Nique was there. This meant that any meaningful conversation between the other Kaxians all took place in Kanx, which Oreo didn't understand because for some odd reason, he didn't have access to his Kaxian memories. I badly wanted to get the others to tell Oreo he was a Kaxian and all us were, too. But it would be a breach of protocol for me to speak to them of such things in the language that the Nique understood, while the Nique was where he could hear us.

My fellow Kaxians said some derogatory things about this particular Nique, really letting him have it, but they spoke in Kanx, so the Nique couldn't understand.

"Come on out of there and say that to our faces, if you're so tough," a male German Shepherd said.

"Yeah, that's right, hide under your human," a female Golden Retriever told the Nique.

"You're not worth a fight, anyway," said a male English Sheep Dog.

"Yeah, there's not even enough of you for a full

meal!" This from a jittery greyhound who could barely keep her feet still, she so wanted to be outside, running.

I had previously noticed that Oreo didn't understand Kanx, and now of course I knew why. I didn't want Oreo to feel left out, so I stayed out of that conversation.

Oreo caught on that I understood the Kanx conversation, though.

I couldn't help chuckling now and then. Some of the things they said were funny!

Anyway, whenever I chuckled, Oreo stared at me for a minute without looking away, not even after I looked away a few times. I knew his look was trying to tell me he was on to me. It made me so sad that he assumed we were up to no good. I could tell that by the disapproving look in his eye when he stared.

I wanted to explain to him this was the big group I belonged to, that we were all Kaxians together and he was, too, and wasn't it great? But that pesky Nique was in here with us, and I'd learned it was pointless trying to win Oreo over where a Nique could hear and sabotage my efforts. I wouldn't be falling for that ploy again.

But these were my fellow Kaxians, and it looked like Oreo and I would be living nearby them, so I thought it best if I introduced us to them. I also figured it would be easier to explain our situation here than in the distance relay system, although I suspected the news would spread through that anyhow, as soon as these Kaxians left the vet's office.

I spoke to them all in Kanx, "Hello. I'm Raffle. My Kaxian name is Clem."

"Hello! I'm Max." The German Shepherd

regarded me calmly. "My Kaxian name is Riffan."

"Hi, Raffle." The Golden Retriever wagged her tail enthusiastically. "I'm Maggie. My Kaxian name is Thres."

"Hiya! I'm Piglet now that this human loves me, but my Kaxian name is Jaha." The English Sheepdog was so big he barely fit on the floor in front of his human mistress. His presence made it doubly silly that the Nique was claiming the territory. The Nique knew we wouldn't do anything to him with all these humans here. He was taking advantage of this opportunity to act all big. Get it? He was really small, and he was acting like he was big!

"I'm Blue, Filgn in Kaxian." The greyhound was still jiggling her legs in place, itching to be out running.

"I'm very pleased to meet you all, Max, Maggie, Piglet, and Blue. Ferd here is my new adopted brother."

At the sound of his Kaxian name, Oreo's ears went up. This whole time he had been staring at me with the most awful look on his face, like he was accusing me of being in a gang and selling drugs, because I was using slang. I hated that he thought that of me, but I really did need to reach out to our fellow Kaxians while I had the chance. But now I knew that he knew his Kaxian name. I could use that later!

Max, Maggie, Piglet, and Blue all smiled at Oreo and said hello, not realizing he couldn't understand them.

I continued to address our new Kaxian friends. "Yeah, he doesn't understand Kanx."

They looked at me with puzzled expressions on their faces.

"He doesn't know he's a Kaxian."

They started to talk, but I just kept talking. I didn't want to draw this out longer than it had to take. I knew poor Oreo was feeling left out, even though he was concentrating on calling me a hypocrite, with his eyes.

"And he isn't bonded with our humans, but I've been calling him Oreo like they do, on account of him not knowing he's a Kaxian. But now I see that he does know his Kaxian name, so that gives me someplace to start in my task of making him understand he's a Kaxian."

Max lay down and put his nose on top of his paws. "Whew. You have your work cut out for you, Raffle."

Blue's feet kept jiggling, which made her whole body bounce up and down when she turned to me and asked, "What part of town are you living in now?"

When I told my new Kaxian friends where Oreo and I lived, I saw shock on their faces.

"What?"

Everyone looked at Max to explain it to me, I guess because he was the oldest of us. "Well, that is the Nique side of town."

My brow scrunched up. "Wait. The Niques have a 'side of town'?"

Max's ears went down slowly. He was still lying down, but he raised his head slightly. "The Niques kind of rule that area. Mostly they live there. We don't patrol over that way."

"Piglet?"

A vet's assistant wearing a white lab coat had come out of a door and was calling Piglet and his human to come inside to see the doctor.

"Bye Everyone! It was nice meeting you all!" Piglet's long hair hung in his eyes, but I thought he meant it. He seemed cheery.

"Bye, Piglet!" We all raised our noses to him.

Maggie blinked at me in a friendly way. "Of course the message relay will reach where you live, though, so if you need anything, you can ask any of us."

"Yeah."

"We'll fix you up."

"Just ask."

Oreo had finally gotten bored with staring at me in that way that said he accused me of being a hypocrite because I knew slang. He had calmed down a little, too. His mind wasn't blue yet, but it was more a purple than red with anger, as it had been a few minutes ago. I composed a little mental movie of him snoozing and sent it his way. Might as well minimize his distress.

A minute later, Oreo was snoring. Loudly. And farting like he always does when he sleeps.

Maggie and Blue giggled every time Oreo farted.

Max covered his nose with his paws. I knew from experience that wasn't going to help any with the awful odor of an Oreo fart.

Max said to me, "Be listening to the relay for any Kaxian duty we might have for you too, of course."

I smiled at Max. "Of course. I will."

"Blue?" The vet's assistant called out.

It was Blue's turn to say bye to us all, which she did, with her legs still twitching.

"Bye Blue!"

This whole time, the little Weiner Dog Nique was

giving us grief from under his human's legs. I'd been hoping the vet's assistant would call him in so that Oreo could meet Max at least, and maybe even Maggie, but then two more Niques came in from the parking lot with their human. She was an elderly lady in a mint green suit, and they were both female toy poodles. They listened to their Weiner Dog buddy for a minute to get the gist of his program of harassment, and then they joined in his campaign to mouth off at us.

"Human!" Poodle #1 pulled on her pink rhinestone leash until she was around one of the legs of the wooden bench.

"Look! Danger!" Poodle #2 pulled on her yellow rhinestone leash in the opposite direction around the bench leg.

The two of them hopped around and cried out and spun around each other so much, they were making me tired even though I had closed my eyes and just had to hear them.

"Raffle and Oreo?"

My human answered the vet's assistant.

"Yep, that's us!"

"We're ready for you now. Come on back!"

I elbowed Oreo awake and called out "Bye!" to Maggie and Max.

"Bye Raffle," Max said. "Bye, Oreo."

"Nice meeting you!"

Oreo's ears perked up at the sound of his name, but he didn't turn toward my new friends. He was still grumpy.

We both got a routine exam and a clean bill of health, and then inspiration struck me from Kax. I composed a very short mental movie and put it in my male human's mind, causing him to ask the vet a very important question:

"So, how old is Oreo, anyway?"

"He's about three years old."

"What?"

"Oreo here? He's about three years old."

"But look, he doesn't have any teeth in the back."

Oreo was shaking a bit as he allowed our female human to open his mouth and show the vet his lack of rear teeth. He avoided my gaze, which told me he knew he was done lording over me. Finally!

The vet explained to our humans matter-of-factly but kindly, "No he doesn't have any rear teeth, but that's just his breed, not a sign of puppy-hood. Springer Spaniels are bred for hunting, and they bring game back to their masters in the backs of their mouths. The lack of teeth has been bred into him so that he doesn't damage game."

Oreo just stood there gently wagging his tail and looking at each of our humans in turn, waiting to see if they would get angry with him.

Of course they didn't. How would they know what he'd been doing to me, lording it over me about being a puppy that I needed to care for? Humans aren't very observant or perceptive. They don't notice the subtleties of interaction. They are very dependent on us.

I was starting to despair of ever leading Oreo to accept that he was a Kaxian! Everything I tried failed. Well, I hadn't tried praying to Kax yet. So I tried that, finally.

Kax gave me advice that surprised me, but now that I stopped to think, it shouldn't have. I had been trying to bring Oreo into my world. I needed to go meet him where he was, and I needed to do it as a friend, as an equal. All this time, I had been acting like I really was a big brother who thought he knew better than Oreo.

Chapter 23: Baj

Baj, Mof, Tef, Gat, Pim, Cor, Elp, and Sah were happy. Their humans had installed a doggy door! This meant they were free to go work on their tunnel in the middle of the night, when the new Kaxians next door were least likely to be in their yard. However, when it came to the cats who hung out in that yard, the middle of the night was the most dangerous time. Their parents were showing them a new way to approach their tunnel, to help them avoid being eaten by the cats.

Parents being along meant no singing out their numbers when they were first, second, or third to go under the fence. They probably shouldn't do this in the middle of the night anyway, but with parents along, they didn't dare. Baj and Mof didn't dare fight to see who went under the fence first.

They had to think of new ways to have fun, and so far that meant making funny faces at each other whenever Mom and Dad weren't looking. Pim made the funniest faces, so Baj usually looked toward her. There was a great face!

Mom cleared her throat.

With a guilty face, Baj turned back toward where Mom was giving a boring lecture on their side of the hole under the fence.

195

"We'll go in a single file line, biggest to littlest. As soon as we go under the fence, we'll turn left. We'll follow the fence to the house. Then, we'll follow the house to the fence on the other side of the yard, which we'll follow to the tunnel..."

Baj drifted off into a daydream of himself out in the middle of the neighbor's backyard in the daytime, running toward the shed. He was bigger, fully grown, so he was on his own.

One of the cats dropped down out of the tree in front of him.

Baj wasn't afraid. Switching on his super Nique speed, he ran through the hole in the side of the shed that was too small for the cat to follow.

The cat's head hit the side of the shed with a satisfactory *bang*.

The inside of the shed was a dream come true! Food wrappers lay strewn everywhere, with ample leftovers stuck to them. Baj gorged himself on the discarded remains of tacos, hamburgers, French fries, and even a few salads with those crispy tortilla chips in them. He got to feeling so confident, maybe he'd go out there and fight that cat. Yeah, he'd...

"Baj! Baj! Baj!"

He finally heard his mother yelling his name when his father nipped him on the nose. He shook his head. "Sorry, Mom."

"This is serious business, Baj! Those cats are just waiting for you to zone out so they can grab you and eat you! You must pay attention and keep up with the rest of us, for your own good!"

"Yes, Mom." Baj fell into place between Mof and Tef, in front of the rest of their litter of puppies.

In a single-file line, Dad led them all to the left

along the fence.

Mof turned around and gave Baj a scary face.

Baj had to puff his cheeks out to not laugh! He turned around and showed Tef the funny face. A few seconds later, he heard Cor giggling at Pim's version of the face. He wished he could see it. It was probably the funniest one.

Dad turned to the right and led them to the house and under the back door of the house.

An owl hooted, and they all froze in fear.

When they didn't hear any more hoots, Dad led around to the left of the house and to the opposite fence until they finally reached their tunnel.

Moonlight shone off shiny bits of the rocks on the ground. They had hours and hours to dig before the humans should wake up and let the Kaxians who now lived here out into this yard.

The tunnel was just big enough for two of the Chihuahua puppies to enter side by side, but it also just barely allowed Dad to enter.

"Let me see your handiwork, children! All of you, follow me! Mom, you stay in the back."

All ten of them raced to the bottom of the tunnel.

Baj wondered why Dad was taking them down there when they would just have to back all the way up. The tunnel was too narrow for them to turn around. When Dad stopped at the end of the tunnel, Baj heard a computer voice speaking in the adult language Mom and Dad had been talking in the other day when he and Mof made everyone be quiet so they could all listen.

"Identify," the computer voice said.

Baj glanced at Mof next to him.

Mof made a funny face.

Yes, it was dark in the tunnel, but their eyes were full of light from the moon. They could see just fine.

Mof pulled his bottom lip back, revealing his bottom teeth. He didn't have any idea what was going on.

Baj tried peeking under Dad's belly to see what was going on up front at the end of the tunnel.

Blue light was shining out of the end of the tunnel, around Dad's paws, which he had placed up in front of him. There was a clicking noise, and then a waft of air blew Baj and Mof's fur back.

All the puppies behind them gasped when they felt the air. Mom, too.

"What was that?" Pim asked in her sweet girlie voice.

"Shall we go see?" Dad said. His voice sounded like when he asked if they wanted to go outside and play.

"Yes!" They all screamed, running after him into where the air had wafted from, tails wagging as fast as they could.

Once they were all inside, a clicking noise sounded, and the air stopped leaving into the tunnel. Baj looked over where the tunnel should be, and two smooth metal doors had closed there.

He looked all around. He was in a room that held all 10 of them with space for 20 more Niques. Everything was made of plastic and metal. There were several doors with paw places in them like where Dad's paw had opened the front door. The ceiling was pretty high, a whole foot over his Chihuahua puppy head.

Baj figured any Nique could fit in here, but he snickered at the thought of some of the bigger

Kaxians trying to slink inside. The door would be a tight fit for either of his new neighbors, Raffle or Oreo. He'd seen a Saint Bernard once, and he didn't think one of those Kaxians could make it in through the door, even if they expanded the tunnel.

"What is this place?" Tef asked Dad.

"This is one of our original space ships from when we first arrived from Nique. We used to go in and out of it easily. This area was all empty high desert for miles around until the humans dammed up the Mojave River and then quickly settled this region in the 1970s."

All the other puppies had gathered around while Dad was talking.

Sah looked around and jumped up with excitement. "This is a spaceship?"

Dad nosed Sah back into the semicircle of sitting puppies and waited until she sat down between Elp and Mof. "Yes, from before we started using space shuttles. 500 Niques came to Earth on this ship."

"Can it still fly?" Elp's tail was wagging extra fast.

Dad sat up straight and smiled. "The humans have settled on top of it, so today we can't fly it even if it works. But that's why you've dug the tunnel to this ship. Kids, you are going to test it out and see what's working."

All the puppies looked around at each other with big silly grins on their faces.

"We would have dug faster if we'd known we were digging up a spaceship!" Gat said.

Sah ran over to Mom to include her in the excitement.

Mom had on a headset and was busy talking into its microphone in that adult language they all understood but were not expected to speak. "Yes," she said into the microphone, "we're inside and as you can hear, the power is on…"

Sah jumped around in front of Mom a few times, but there was no reaction, so she made her way back to Dad.

He stood up. "Well, our first order of business is to inspect and inventory the entire ship. Who wants to go along to do that?" He smiled at them all.

"Me!"

"I do!"

"Me!

"Ooh! Let's go!"

Everyone chimed in, making the nearly empty metal room echo with a cacophony of enthusiasm.

Dad lowered his head and laughed, wagging his tail. "OK, come on!"

Mom stayed and talked on the headset, but all 8 puppies ran off after Dad when he put his paw up on the wall opposite where they came in and it opened an elevator-style double sliding metal door.

They were in a circular hallway that curved away from them to the left and the right. It was big enough for four of them to walk side by side.

Dad turned to the right, and all the puppies followed him.

Metal doors dotted the hallway on both sides every ten feet or so.

"Where do all these doors go?" Cor looked at the first door and kept bending her knees toward it.

"That's what we need to find out!" Dad sat down next to Cor.

"Well, then we better start going inside them, shouldn't we?" Cor took a step toward the door.

Dad laughed and put his paw on the wall next to it.

The first room was full of tall metal boxes with blinky lights in them. Some of the boxes had TV screens. Others had controls Baj thought he would be able to manipulate with his paws.

Dad spoke softly into a tiny headset Baj hadn't noticed he was wearing.

"Room 1, Control."

Then Dad had them all go up to the computer screen and stare into it for a few minutes while resting their front paws on some screens nearby.

"This will make it so you can enter and operate the spaceship without me or Mom."

Mof looked at Baj with a huge grin on his face.

Baj knew how hard it was for Mof to be on such good behavior for so long, not lording it over the littler puppies. Baj understood because it was hard for him, too. He so wanted to fight with Mof over who would make it through the next door first! He didn't dare do that with Dad right there with them.

They followed Dad around, helping him inventory and test all the rooms. There were ordinary rooms for sleeping and for preparing food. There was the engine room, which Gat found particularly interesting with its complex machinery. There were meeting rooms and entertainment rooms. Dad showed them where to put their paws to test all the equipment, and everything worked. He softly spoke each room's purpose and contents into his tiny headset.

The last room they explored was the big one in the center. They had to go up a ramp. Once they got up there, Baj noted that all the center doors led to it.

Elp gasped. "This is so cool!"

It was. They were in the raised center section that controlled the space ship. There were twenty work stations, and every one of them looked out a window. All of these now faced dirt and rocks, but Baj could imagine looking through them into outer space. It gave him chills.

Mom came in and joined them in here, still talking on her own headset, but smiling at all her puppies.

Dad wagged his tail wildly and perked his ears way up. "OK, kids! Pick a work station, all of you!"

Mof and Baj both picked the same station, both wiggling their stomachs onto the lying pad and trying to get their noses into the control sniffer.

Dad growled at them. "Baj, go choose another station."

Once all the puppies were settled into stations, Dad showed them all how to log in to the ship's computer. They learned how to bring up the ship's control programs.

Cor said, "This is really cool, but when are we ever going to use it?"

Dad grinned the biggest grin ever. "You'll use it every night! Kids! This ship is going to teach you all how to fly space shuttles!"

All the little Chihuahua puppies jumped up at that exciting news, tails wagging a mile a minute, ears perked up, and tongues hanging out of their mouths.

Sah took their excitement one step further. "Yay! We're gonna fly space shuttles! Mom, did you hear that?" She ran over to Mom and kept running around and around her. "We're gonna fly, Mom! We're gonna fly!"

Mom smiled at Sah and licked her nose. And then she covered the microphone with her paw. "I know, Sah! Isn't it great?"

She had to be quick about that, because whoever she was talking to wanted a response right away.

Chapter 24: Oreo

Great. That stupid vet had spilled the beans. The humans knew I was not a puppy. They stopped telling Uptight Dog to clean the wax out of my ears. They ruined my fun! Oh well. I was not going to stick around here anyway. First chance I got, I was going to run away and never come back.

In the meantime though, I was going to have some fun. The real fun in life is hunting. At least, for me it is. I never feel more alive than when I'm chasing after my prey. It's all about the chase. That vet was right about one thing: Springer Spaniels like me are made for the hunt.

There were all kinds of prey critters in the back yard of our new den: lizards, rabbits, birds of all types, snakes, the occasional cat... but mostly gophers. The place was infested with gophers. Actually, I wondered why the humans had decided to make their den on top of a gopher colony and then spray lots of water all over the grass that gophers love to eat! That was not a smart thing to do. Sometimes I wonder if humans are going to survive much longer; they can be so stupid.

We Springer Spaniels are mostly bird dogs. We're good at jumping into the water and swimming over to get birds that fall in when you shoot them. Our coats are thick, so thick that it takes a long time for water to soak through and get our skin wet. This comes in handy because birds often fly over water, and people hunt them in the fall when the weather is getting colder.

Gophers burrow under the ground, as you probably know. I'm too big to burrow in after them. That's what terrier dogs are for. "Terrier" is Latin for "earth digger." Are you surprised I know that? Heh. Yeah, I'm a country bumpkin who is ignorant about most of your city type things, but hunting is something I know a lot about. I do when it comes to dogs hunting, anyway.

But just because I wasn't a terrier and I couldn't burrow in after the gophers didn't mean I couldn't get 'em. They couldn't stay down there in their hidey hole all the time. Yeah, their burrow probably went down to the water table, so they didn't have to come up for water, and they could pull the grass down to them by the roots, so they didn't need to come up for food. But they wanted other food. Mostly what was available for them was the grass. At least the humans hadn't planted carrots, radishes, turnips, onions, or any other food that grew underground! Only a terrier would be able to get the gophers in that case.

This new den our humans had moved us to didn't have a doggy door, either. For the first couple weeks, we still had to beg to be let outside. Our female human worked from home, though. She was on the phone most of the day, for business, and didn't want to bother opening and closing the door for us. It was spring, so neither the heater nor the air conditioner was on. This worked in our favor because finally she decided to just leave the back door open and let us come and go as we pleased during her working hours. She did close the door to the rest of the humans' den so that we only tracked dirt into that one room.

I was so happy at this relative freedom that I almost decided to stay here with these nice humans. Almost. But I did decide to have some fun hunting while I waited for my chance to dig out and leave. Uptight Dog had to fall asleep during the day at some point. He couldn't always be watching me, just waiting for me to try to dig out so he could go tell his human on me. I was just biding my time until that happened.

All day long while the female human worked and the back door stood open, I camped outside the main entrance to the gophers' underground warren of tunnels. From up here, it just looked like a hole in the ground with a mound of dirt piled up next to it, but I could smell dozens of different gophers down there. I could hear them talking to each other in their high-pitched, squeaky voices.

"Put your grass over here."

"Go get more grass!"

"Hey! That's my grass!"

"We need more grass!"

"Can't we eat something else?"

They made no mention of me, so I figured they were clueless to my predatory intent. I could hear them scampering around. I could hear them gnawing on the roots of the grass, pulling the grass down into their tunnel, and then spitting it out of the pouches in their cheeks, deep inside their den. I could even hear them breathing.

I was waiting for a gopher to come out, so I could catch it. Plenty of things tried to distract me. Those aggressive dogs out back, Roy and Ocho, kept telling me I better stay out of their yard.

"We'll eat you if you come over here!"

"Better stay on your side of the alley!"

The Rottweilers to the west of us weren't much nicer, but at least they didn't threaten to eat me.

"You better stay on your side of the fence."

"We can't ensure your safety, if you come over here."

The cute German Shepherd puppies and their pretty blue-eyed mother in the yard right behind ours tempted me to come over and check on them.

"Buddy! Over here!"

"I got the ball!"

"Bring it this way, Brownie!"

But my biggest distraction was all the Chihuahua dogs that lived east of us. The trouble was, those eight Chihuahua puppies didn't want to stay on their side of the fence! The dirt here was dry and flaky. It was easy to dig under the fence. Any dog could come into our yard if they really wanted to, and for some dumb reason, the 8 little Chihuahua puppies did want to.

I wouldn't have cared that they came over into our yard, except that they alerted the gophers to my menacing presence. I'm sure they did it on purpose! The Chihuahuas had their own slang, so I couldn't really understand what they were yipping about, but it's hard to imagine anyone being so annoying by accident. The only way to get rid of them, short of killing them of course, was for me to yell at them long enough that the female human noticed, even though she was on the phone for her work.

Over and over again, the Chihuahua puppies

would come into our yard. Over and over again, the three of us: Uptight Dog, the female human, and I, we would chase those Chihuahua puppies down, catch them, and return them to their humans—only to have them scramble under the fence and start the whole process again.

The gophers couldn't help but hear us yelling to each other as we chased those little Chihuahuas all over the place.

"One went that way!"

"Now it's over here!"

"Don't let it run out the open gate!"

"Why not?"

"It'll run into the street!"

"So?"

I guess chasing and catching the Chihuahuas might have been more fun than hunting the gophers. Unlike the gophers, who stayed underground in their warren of tunnels most of the time, at least the Chihuahuas were out in the open where we could actually catch them. Catching them was fun. Maybe it was fun for them, too. Why else would they keep coming into our yard?

But the Chihuahuas weren't always in the yard. Some of the time, I actually was waiting by the gopher hole, hoping one of the gophers would come up so I could get it.

Uptight Dog must have been really bored without his friends around. He started trying to hang out with me while I was waiting for the gophers to come out. I explained to him over and over that I didn't want the gophers to know I was there and so we had to be quiet, but he just didn't listen.

Uptight dog was almost as annoying as the

Chihuahua puppies. What a joke that the humans had thought he could be my big brother. He was more than a year old, but he was like a little puppy!

"How's it going?" he'd ask me.

"Shh! You'll scare the gophers!"

A few minutes went by.

"Look at all the birds flying by!" he'd say.

"Shh! You'll scare the gophers!"

A few minutes later:

"Isn't it funny how those Chihuahuas want to be in our yard?"

"Shh! You'll scare the gophers!"

Finally, Uptight Dog was quiet for long enough and the Chihuahuas stayed away long enough that a gopher came out!

I let it get all the way out and some distance away before I moved even a bit. I didn't want to give it a chance to back down into the burrow.

Know what makes a gopher back down? Gopher burrows are so narrow, they don't have room to turn around; that's what! A little hunting humor.

A gopher slowly crept toward the yummy seeds hidden in a nearby pine cone, cautiously looking all about. It looked up just as often as it looked around. Cats might jump out of the trees, and there were crows and hawks that could sweep out of the sky and grab a gopher in seconds. That would be OK with me! This was my territory, for now, anyway, and I wanted the gophers out. The crows and the hawks wouldn't move in, but the cats might, so I did my best to keep them away, too.

Once that gopher was busy plucking seeds out of the pine cone, I crawled very slowly on my knees and elbows until I was close enough to pounce on it.

Crawling put less of me in the sun, so my shadow wasn't as long. My shadow would have given me away. Once I got close enough, I pounced on the gopher and finished it.

Uptight Dog was impressed.

"Wow! You got it! That was incredible! Can you teach me how to do that?"

He meant it. There was no sarcasm in his tone at all.

I wasn't ready for that. In my mind, the two of us were enemies. He stood for the humans and captivity and the cage and everything I wanted to run away from. That was why I resisted every time he suggested anything. Up to now, all his suggestions had been about behaving the way the humans wanted us to.

This was the first time my 'brother' talked about doing anything that I even remotely wanted to do.

I didn't have a response ready because I never expected such an uptight dog to take any interest in anything fun! And I could tell he was really interested in learning how to hunt.

His tail was wagging; his ears were perked up; his tongue was even hanging out of his mouth, he was so excited. His excitement was contagious, so without really thinking about it, I just agreed to teach him.

"Yeah, I could teach you."

"Awesome! Can we start now?"

"Yeah. Let's back off from this lawn this way over here."

"Why don't we just go back where you were before?"

"Because now our scent is over there."

"Oh yeah."

"Yeah. We don't want our scent to get too strong

in any one location."

"Wow, there's much more to this hunting stuff than I realized!"

"It all makes sense once you realize it's all about stealth."

"Heh! Yeah, we herding dogs don't have much use for stealth!"

"Heh! Not unless you're hunting for your dinner, no, I guess you don't!"

The weirdest thing happened then. The two of us sat there smiling at each other! The second weirdest thing that happened was that he actually waited quietly for the next gopher to come out.

Oh, he wasn't completely cured of being an excited little pup. He would get the urge to say something every few seconds. I could tell because his head would jerk up and he would open his mouth to say something, but now he controlled himself. Instead of saying anything, he would just smile at me, wag his tail, and hunker down to watch the gopher hole.

Three Chihuahua invasions and four gopher runs later, he caught a gopher all by himself.

"I did it!"

"Yeah, you did!"

"I can't believe it!"

"I'm having trouble believing it, myself."

"Why? You're a great teacher."

"I am, aren't I?"

Things were different between us after that. For one thing, I quit calling him Uptight Dog. I called him Raffle, because that was what he wanted me to call him.

Chapter 25: Raffle

I was finally making progress with Oreo! As an added bonus, hunting was fun! I had not expected that. I don't know why not. I should have realized there was a reason that Oreo liked hunting. But until I tried it, I assumed it was going to be drudgery that I would have to put up with in order to do my duty to Kax.

The two of us had a good old time. We kept all the birds, squirrels, and snakes from moving into our yard. And they did try. Do you doubt we were able to deter the birds? They did spend most of their time in the trees, but most of the seeds they wanted to eat dropped down to the ground, where they'd have to come and peck them up with their bobbly heads while walking about on their little bird legs.

"The trick is to sneak up on them while they're busy with their seeds," Oreo said.

"Sneak up on them?"

"Yeah."

I said, "I don't know if you've noticed, but I have long legs meant for running. They are not good legs for sneaking!"

"You could sneak, if you wanted to," Oreo said.

"How do you expect me to sneak? Fold my legs up under me like the cat when she's sleeping?"

"Hey, that would work."

I looked at him, waiting for him to laugh, but Oreo was serious. He really thought I had a chance at sneaking up on the birds, so I tried it. The next time there was a bird in our yard, I stopped chasing the Chihuahuas and folded my legs up under me like a cat.

"That's good," Oreo whispered, "Now stay low like that, so your shadow doesn't tell the bird you're there, and creep up on the bird till you can pounce on it."

Well, creeping up on a bird with your legs folded up under you is hard! I tried, but I looked like a fish trying to sneak up on a bird! My body was flailing around all over the place on the grass. Nah. That wasn't my style. I'm the sophisticated type.

"You sneak up on it!" I whispered back.

"OK. Watch so you can do it next time."

Oreo was shorter than me. All he had to do was squat a little to avoid having his shadow give him away. He got the bird in three seconds flat.

I had an idea, though. I noted where the sun was and where the shadows were falling so that I could always hang out on the side of the yard where I wouldn't cast a shadow. The next time there was a bird in our yard, I didn't have to fold my legs under me. My shadow was behind me. I crouched just the way Oreo had, and I got that bird!

"Good job, Raffle!" Oreo said.

Yeah, he and I were getting along really well now.

Life in service to Kax is never boring, though. Just when it looked like I had the problem of getting along with Oreo wrapped up, Kax dropped another one in my lap.

See, just like Oreo, neither the puppies that lived

214

behind us nor their mother knew they were Kaxians, either. How had this been allowed to happen? Why hadn't those puppies' mother's mother told her that she was a Kaxian? That was every Kaxian parent's duty: to raise up good Kaxian puppies who understood their duty to Kax and asked Kax for guidance.

After a while, I realized that I myself had not been asking Kax for guidance as often as I should. I'm one of few Kaxians who can speak with and hear Kax at will, so it was especially stupid of me not to. I remedied that right in the moment.

I opened my mind to Kax. There was the usual reassurance that I was not alone, that help and guidance were always there, just waiting for me to ask. Through our planet's collective consciousness, I got reassurance that all my friends from back in my old neighborhood were well, and that even when they left this life they were all in good standing to be reborn. They would be told that I missed them and loved them, but that I was settling in at my new home, so they needn't worry about me.

Inside this reassurance, I finally asked.

"Kax, how do I approach Oreo and tell him he's a Kaxian so that the memories will come back to him? I've tried everything I can think of. He scoffs at me whenever I try to tell him anything. He's older than me, this life. He wasn't interested in being friends with Lido or anyone from the old neighborhood and hearing it from them so it wasn't from me. War with the Niques doesn't even get his dander up. He doesn't see them as they truly are: our rivals. The only thing he likes is hunting, and I don't see how that helps us any."

I heard responses coming, but I wanted to get my apologies in, first. The collective consciousness determined who would be reborn and who would die forever. It was best to stay on its good side!

"I am so sorry for letting this go on so long. In my pride, I was sure I could bring him around, that I knew what was best, and that my special abilities would allow me to convince him easily. I guess I am still a little young and headstrong in this current life. You gave me these abilities to serve you. Please tell me how!"

My apology was received with acceptance and a little amusement.

Kax's answer to the question of what to do about Oreo and the puppies' ignorance really surprised me:

"Keep working on Oreo, and then let him tell the pups and their mother about being Kaxians. You can help move this along by asking Oreo what he has in common with these pups."

Wow. I was afraid to ask Oreo anything. He could be so unpleasant. But the collective consciousness of my entire planet has never been wrong in my experience. They don't always have an answer, but when they do, it's the right answer.

And Oreo did seem to be warming up to me.

So one evening by the fire, after a particularly fun day hunting, I did ask Oreo if he had anything in common with those pups.

"Dang, how could you tell?"

"Ask me that again after you tell me your story."

"You sure want to hear it?"

"Yeah, and how I could tell is a long story in and of itself."

Oreo got the old familiar scowl on his face for a

second, and then his face relaxed. He looked into my eyes for a few moments, and then he relaxed even more.

"I have a lot in common with those puppies. Have you talked to them at all?"

"No. No, I haven't."

"Let's go talk to them. I think that'll be... educational for you."

"But it's dark out. They'll be inside by now."

I didn't think Oreo heard me. He was already at the back door, getting one of the humans to let us out. I ran quick and joined him. I was sure our errand would be in vain because the puppies would be inside, but it would be nice to get outside for a few minutes.

The ice had stopped coming at night. It was getting warmer during the day, but at night I was still glad I slept in the house. Bbbrrrr. It was a bit nippy, even with my winter coat.

The sky was clear, though, and the stars were out. They distracted me for a few seconds. I love looking at the starry sky. I gazed off in the direction of Kax. Should I point out Kax's galaxy to Oreo, er, to Ferd?

"Are you coming?"

"Huh? Oh! You still think the puppies are out? It's pretty cold."

"Listen."

Oreo perked his ears up toward the lot north of us.

So, I did the same. I heard the puppies then, crying to their mother.

"Huh. You're right. I guess their humans don't take very good care of the puppies."

Oreo nodded as he trotted off to the north side of our backyard fence.

Except for the yard with the puppies, it was quiet out at this time of night. All the other dogs were inside. Oh, they would bark if anyone—Kaxian, Nique, animal or human—came close to their houses, and they did get let outside to do their business at night, but our new neighborhood was mostly peaceful at night.

When we got closer to the north yard that lay across the dirt alley, we could plainly hear the German Shepherd puppies.

"Brownie! I was there first!"

"So? This is my spot!"

"Says who?'

"This has always been my spot."

"Has not!"

"Has too."

"Not!"

"Has."

"Mom! I can't sleep with Buddy and Brownie shouting like that."

"I can't, either!"

"Make them be quiet!"

They were beautiful puppies. Their mom was mostly a cream color, which is rare in German Shepherds, and she had gorgeous blue eyes. She was rather angry at the moment, and her voice betrayed that, even if her words hadn't.

"I'm about to make you all be quiet!"

What was even worse, the mom Kaxian growled at her pups.

Shocked, I did what I could to stop her from doing violence to her own offspring.

"Excuse me, Ma'am?"

She jumped up and turned her head toward me.

"Who are you calling Ma'am?"

"I'm sorry. I don't know your name."

She raised her nose at me. "It's Buttons."

"Pleased to meet you, Buttons. I'm Raffle, and this is my brother, Oreo."

She looked at me sideways. "Look, I'm sure you're just being friendly, but I'm really busy, in case you couldn't tell."

"We won't take up much of your time. It's just that my brother Oreo thinks he might have something in common with you, and I'm curious what that might be."

She sighed. "Well, unless he was raised in a puppy farm, too, I can't imagine what that might be."

Now, I looked at her sideways. "A puppy farm? What do you mean?"

Then Oreo inexplicably got angry at me.

"For a smart dog, Raffle, you sure can be an idiot sometimes! Don't make her explain that in front of her puppies! Let's go back to the house, pronto."

"Bye, Buttons. It was nice meeting you."

She shook her head no at us. "I guess. Bye."

Our humans were waiting for us at the door. They petted us and gave us each one of those big dog biscuits. We sat there together, each breaking up our dog biscuit so we could chew it up.

Oreo said, "Raffle, I grew up with a single mom, like Buttons, but at least not on a puppy farm. It was a strawberry farm, and we dogs were just there to guard the strawberries. We weren't pets. I was expendable, not a member of the humans' family, the way you are here."

I stopped chewing my dog biscuit. "You mean, you didn't have nice humans around when you were a puppy? You slept outside, like Buttons and her family do?"

"That's right." Oreo lay down and looked up at me with his sad brown eyes. "I was only with my mother three weeks. Not all humans are nice to dogs, Raffle."

"I'm sorry. I'm so sorry that happened to you, Oreo."

I thought I knew this world. Nothing had prepared me for dogs who don't even know they are Kaxians, let alone dogs who only get three weeks with their mothers! What a screwed up world we live in.

I wanted to believe this would ever happen on Kax, but I didn't think I'd ever get to find out. Not during this lifetime, at any rate.

I didn't have a clue what to do, and so again I communed with Kax. At least now the problem was smaller. All I had to ask was how to tell Oreo he was a Kaxian, although now that I thought about it, that was all Kax had ever asked me to do. It was me who kept thinking I had to make friends with Oreo first.

Too bad I wasted so much time trying to make him my friend and do what I wanted to do, rather than being his friend and doing what he liked to do.

I enjoyed the wonderful feeling of belonging and acceptance that Kax always gives me, and I took a minute to check in on Lido and the rest of the pack back in our old neighborhood. They were all fine, and on track to be reborn even if they weren't fine. I felt guilty for a minute at having such a nice home to be able to check in on, when Oreo and our new neighbor puppies had nothing like that.

I got my answer, and I thanked Kax for it.

Chapter 26: Oreo

Raffle's humans were rushing around the house picking things up off the floor, putting things into cupboards, folding up blankets, vacuuming the floor, and wiping everything in the kitchen. I knew what that meant: strange humans were going to invade their den.

I don't think I'll ever understand why humans make their dens nicer when they know invaders are coming. It would make more sense to set up defenses. If I were in charge, of course I wouldn't let any strange humans in, but I certainly wouldn't try to make it nicer for them!

I would put all the food away, for one thing. Silly humans always leave food out where invading humans can get it to eat! Humans who are not in their pack! I wouldn't even have to fight in order to stop invaders from taking food. I wouldn't have food out in the first place. I would bury it all.

Another dumb thing the humans did whenever strangers were going to invade the house was they locked us inside our kennels in their bedroom! How stupid was that? Here we were, the only two actual fighters in the pack, and we got locked up when invaders came. The humans knew I had been abandoned in a kennel, too. But were they

221

understanding? Well, OK, they were, a little bit. I tried to explain to them why locking their fighters in kennels during an invasion was a bad idea.

But of course, they couldn't understand me. And, they were stubborn! They were not going to give up. Once they told us to do something, they made us do it, no matter how long it took.

"Oreo! Go in your house." Our mistress said it sweetly, as if it were an invitation.

I wanted to be pleasant.

Really.

She was so nice to me. She gave me a biscuit whenever I came to the back door after she'd called me. She petted me almost non-stop, except when she was working. She knew just how to scratch under my collar, where I couldn't reach with my hind claws.

But I was not going to volunteer to be locked inside a kennel. Especially not with invaders coming. I lay down in front of the 'house' to show her I understood what she said, and then I wagged my tail to show her I was happy here, thank you very much.

Like I said, she was stubborn. "Go in your house," she said, more sternly.

I pushed my eyebrows together the way she does when the water comes out of her eyes. Her mate always comforts her when that happens, so I hoped that look would make her want to comfort me. I got up and licked her hands, to show her I loved her and wanted her to be happy.

Incidentally, I braced myself by digging my claws into the carpet, against being pushed into the kennel.

As I knew she would, she tried to push me toward the kennel. At first, she pushed gently. When I didn't budge, she grrrrr'd a little and really put her weight behind the push. When I still didn't budge, she said her command again, this time in a decidedly stern voice.

"Oreo, go in your house."

I made the crying noises in my throat—you know, those high-pitched sounds puppies make, the ones that melt humans' hearts—and I licked her hands and arms, all the while bracing myself on the carpet with claws dug in against her pushes.

"Let me," her mate said.

It was pretty much 'game over' then. Without any fuss at all, he picked me up, put me in the kennel, closed the door, and fastened it.

I liked her better.

I couldn't stand it inside the locked kennel! There was nothing to eat! There was no water! I was going to die in here! I had to get out!

Without even meaning to, I burst out yelling.

"Don't leave me in here! I can't stand it! Let me out! I'm scared! Besides, you need me to defend your den from the intruders!"

The humans couldn't understand me, of course. To them, I just sounded like a dog barking nonsense noises. But Raffle understood me. He was actually comforting.

"It'll be OK, Oreo."

"It won't! I'm so afraid!"

"They won't leave us here."

"But what if they do?"

"They know we'll have to find a tree before too long."

"Any time is too long!"

"Just go to sleep. They never let the invaders stay overnight. They're usually gone in four hours, at the most."

"How can you sleep at a time like this?"

"It's easy. Just relax."

I did my best to relax. I really did. I closed my eyes and sprawled on the thick cushion inside the kennel. I took a deep breath. For some strange reason, I actually did start to go to sleep! I was having a great dream about Buttons, that pretty cream-colored German Shepherd mom dog in the lot behind us.

And then the monster came into the bedroom, in real life.

"DOGGIES!" the monster shrieked in a painful pitch, waking me up and making all my fur stand up with goose bumps.

"Wan pet ta DOGGIES!"

The monster came running toward me, small pudgy hands out in front of her, small bowed legs barely keeping her upright.

BAM! BAM! BAM!

The monster banged on my house, trying with all her strength to bash it down and get at me! She meant to do me harm! Who knows what kind of harm, but all the while she kept shrieking in a voice so loud I wished I could plug my ears like humans do on TV.

"Wan pet ta DOGGIES! Doggy play me!"

Her round eye came up close to the wire mesh door of my house and stared in with the wild glint of a hunter.

I knew that look, and I was her prey! I almost make another puddle of pee to stand in, I was so scared.

The monster's chubby fingers grabbed hold of my front door. She tugged on the door so hard, my whole house rocked back and forth. The jerkiness almost made her topple over, but unfortunately for me, she didn't give up. When this didn't open the door, the monster banged on the top of my house some more.

BAM! BAM! BAM!

My house was sturdy plastic. Surely she wouldn't be able to break the door down, even if she huffed and puffed her hardest?

I found myself talking to the door of my house.

"Please don't break. Please stay there and protect me. Please?"

Raffle wasn't very reassuring now.

All the while this was going on, over and over, in an ever-increasingly panicky voice, Raffle kept telling me:

"Don't hurt her, Oreo!"

"Don't hurt her, Oreo!"

"Don't hurt her, Oreo!"

Me not hurt *her*? She was trying her hardest to break into my house so she could tear me apart limb from limb! She was every bit as wild and untamed as those wolves I had faced, out in the wilderness. She hadn't a care for how I felt. It was all about her having fun. She was on the rampage, and deadly.

The monster didn't need a pack to help her hunt me, either. I couldn't do a thing to her. I was helpless. If she got into my house and attacked me, then I would have to just close my eyes and take it like a man. I didn't dare fight her.

She smelled like the humans who had invaded our humans' den, so I knew she was their young. I didn't dare hurt her, or they would kill me. I know not to mess with a larger animal's young. I wasn't born yesterday, you know.

BAM! BAM! BAM!

She squealed another ear-shattering cry, this time without words.

"Eeeeeeeeeeeeeaaaaaaah"

She was pounding so hard on my house that it was bouncing on the carpeted floor! She was only half my size! I now silently thanked my humans for giving me this safe house to hide in, away from the monster. I was so grateful they hadn't left me exposed to whatever she wanted to do to me.

But my house seemed in imminent danger of collapsing under the little monster's attack!

I did the only thing I could do in that situation, besides pee in my house.

I did that, too.

"Kax!" I said in my mind, as Raffle had told me he would do, "I hope you're there, because if you're not, I'm going to die! Help! Keep me safe from this monster! If you keep me safe, then I'll believe you exist!"

I closed my eyes and did my best to "connect" to Kax, the way I had seen Raffle do.

Kax was there!

I felt a calmness come over me. My heart slowed to a normal beat. I quit panting. My tail came out from between my legs and quit its nervous jiggling. My ears went back up. My mind calmed, too.

I saw then that Kax had been protecting me all along. Kax had seen to it that I was rescued from the abandoned crate and adopted by humans who would connect me to fellow Kaxians.

I realized that I was safe with these humans, that they loved me even though I had been nothing but a rascal to them. I didn't need to run away. I had a nice home with a backyard full of stuff to hunt right here, along with a great brother who had also put up with a lot from me.

The humans deserved my love and protection, not only for adopting me in the first place, but for putting up with me chewing the seatbelt and not listening to their commands and pulling on the leash whenever they tried to walk with me and chasing cats and squirrels instead of playing with them in the park.

I made a decision right then to change my ways, to get along with the humans and return some of the love they were so freely giving me. To protect them instead of giving them grief all the time.

The monster was still there, banging on my house and screeching so loud I thought my ears were going to catch fire.

BAM! BAM! BAM!

"Wan pet ta DOGGIES!"

But I somehow knew Kax wouldn't let the monster get me. For the first time in my life, I felt truly safe.

"Thank you, Kax. I owe you my life."

Raffle seemed to relax then, too.

"Welcome back to us, Ferd! I'm so glad you're back!"

My ears perked up at the sound of my old name.

"How do you know my Ferd name?"

"Kax told me."

My eyes must have gotten as big as saucers, because Raffle rushed on to explain.

"Praying to Kax isn't about being 'holy' or putting on a show. We communicate that way. It's a relationship, and communication goes both ways."

Then I remembered the head Rottweiler who had

rescued me calling me Ferd, too, and I knew it was all true. I really was part of a big pack that included every large dog on Earth and many on other planets throughout the universe. That was huge! My mind was expanding. I could feel memories right on the edge of my mind, waiting to come to me, like when a word is right on the tip of your tongue.

Just then, Raffle's male human came in and rescued us from the monster.

"She's in here!"

A male human intruder came in.

"Sweetie, come on out here and have some spaghetti with us!"

That got her attention. She ran to him, and they both went down the hall toward the kitchen.

"Scetti! Scetti!" she screeched out in her high-pitched voice.

Raffle's male human came over and stroked my nose through the grate of my safe house.

"I hear you stopped barking. That's a good boy, Oreo. It's OK. Yeah. You're safe in here. They'll be gone soon. You're OK."

He went over and petted Raffle, too.

"Good boy! Quiet."

Raffle licked his master's fingers, and then the man left the room, closing the door behind him. Just as he promised, the human intruders left soon after that, and our human and his mate let us out of our houses.

"Aw," our human's mate said, "Oreo, I'm sorry we kept you in your house too long. Here, let me clean that up." She went and got rags and cleaned up my puddle of pee.

That did it. I was so touched that she cared about how clean my house was! I rushed to her and licked her arm, to show my gratitude.

She laughed because it tickled, and she scratched the fur under my collar and cooed at me, "Aw, what a love you are!"

And just like that, we bonded.

Chapter 27: Raffle

I'd considered my work done, once Oreo knew he was a Kaxian and had agreed to quit running away from our humans. I'd done my duty to Kax, so I thought. No one's duty is ever done, though. That's a good thing, or we'd all laze around all day and get bored. I would rather be busy than bored. Wouldn't you?

Oreo nipped my ear as he ran by on his way to the back door.

"C'mon! Let's go see Buttons!"

"Alright," I told him, "but you don't have to bite me."

"Heh, just because we're fellow Kaxians doesn't mean I'm not your elder. I think you should treat me with a little more respect!"

Ooh! He actually made me mad! Why had I expected Oreo's personality to change, once he knew he was a Kaxian? He made it perfectly clear he was still going to be difficult! I had to admit he'd spoken the truth, though.

"True. You are my elder. I'll be more respectful from now on."

There. That was a suitable tone for me to take with an elder. I smiled at Oreo, thinking he would now be happy.

But he took a deep breath and rolled his eyes.

"Oh, Brother! Did anyone ever say you take the fun out of everything, Raffle?"

It was my turn to sigh.

"Not in this life, but yes, plenty of times. I never have understood why."

Our mistress came to the back door then and looked at us each in turn for longer than usual. She scratched under both of our collars, one of us with each hand.

We wagged our tails.

She said, "What's gotten into you guys? I don't see any intruders in the backyard. Is everything all right?"

We both looked at her and smiled, wagging our tails, and then looked at the back door.

"OK! OK! I see. You want to outside and play. Here you go!"

We both licked her hand to thank her for opening the door, and then out we ran. I noticed that Oreo made sure he went out first so he could pee on the tree first. After I did the same, he went over mine. He sure was aggressive. I knew that went with him being part Springer Spaniel this life. They are made for hunting, and hunting is aggressive.

Still, I didn't think I would ever quite get used to Oreo's aggression. It was foreign to me, coming from a line of herders.

"Buttons!" Oreo called out, "We're coming for a visit!"

She was a little more friendly this time. I'm guessing it was because we were coming in broad daylight instead of when she wished she were sleeping.

Oreo was over-the-top friendly, though. He ran to her at full speed, his ears and his tail up as high as they would go. He stopped at our back fence and talked to her over the dirt alley.

"Buttons! Raffle knows a bunch of stories that your puppies just have to hear before… you know." His ears and tail went down when he said that. He even whined just a little at the end.

All three of us knew her puppies would soon be sold off to other humans. Oreo was right. If they didn't hear the stories from me before that happened, then they might never hear them this life. And then their own puppies wouldn't hear the Kaxian stories, either. And so on.

"Hi, puppies. I'm Raffle. If it's OK with your mom, I would like to tell you some stories about my pack and the larger pack we come from. I know your pack comes from them, too."

I was relieved that our Nique neighbors were inside. I would still be doing this if, no, when they came out, but it sure was a lot easier to do without them harping on me. Especially since they all seemed determined to keep Oreo and other Kaxians from remembering they were Kaxians.

Buttons looked at me with her eyebrows scrunched together, but she gave her permission and even introduced her pups to me.

"I don't understand why you're bothering, but I'm glad for the company, Raffle. Puppies, stand up when I say your name, so Raffle will know who's who:"

"Buddy!" The largest of the four puppies stood up with his tongue hanging out of his mouth and took a good look at me across the dirt alley and through the two chain-link fences.

"Brownie!" She twirled around after she got up. She had pretty blue eyes like her mama.

"Bonnie!" She stood in place, her tail under her belly.

"Bella!" The smallest puppy's tongue hung out of her mouth, too, just like her brother's.

While she introduced the pups to me, I put my nose right up next to the fence so they could all see how earnest I was in telling this story. It was the one story they really needed to hear before they were taken off to their various other humans' homes. That could happen any time now. They were weaned already. I'd been a fool not to think of it before. I made a mental note to thank Oreo later.

I also sought out the minds of our Nique neighbors. They were all blue with contentment at just having eaten. I composed a mental movie of sleep and sent it to all 10 of them. I felt their minds drift off into sleep. Whew!

I addressed Buttons and her puppies.

"The humans call me Raffle, but my Kaxian name is Clem. I got it when I was born the first time. Do you know what a planet is, Bonnie?"

I looked at Buttons when I said this. She shook her head no.

Bonnie spoke up.

"No, what is a planet?"

"The ground beneath us is the planet Earth. Earth travels in space around the sun. The sun is a star out in space. Space is the blackness you see above you at night. All the other stars in the sky are suns. Some of the other suns have planets that travel around them. I come from a planet called Kax, and so do all of you!"

Again, I looked at Buttons. She wasn't telling me

to go away, which I thought was a really good sign that things were going to be OK.

Brownie said, "But how did we get here, if we're from another planet?"

"Yeah, how?" Bella said.

"We came here on space ships a thousand dog lives ago," I said.

"Where are the space ships now?" Buddy asked.

"Our space ships are deep under the ground. We use them as local headquarters for meetings, ceremonies, and keeping informed about news from Kax," I said.

"Wow! This is a great story!" Bonnie said, "Isn't it, Momma?" She looked up at Buttons with her ears perked up and her tail wagging.

Buttons licked her head. "Yes, this is a great story. Let's pay good attention to Raffle as he tells it. I think I've heard it before. It is starting to sound familiar to me."

Oreo had backed up far enough that he now came running at me, saying, "I don't think there's enough action in this story!" He play growled and pounced on me, much as my brothers and sisters used to do when we were still small and used to play in imitation of the hunting dogs in our neighborhood back home.

For the first time, Oreo's aggression didn't scare me. I trusted that he was playing and wouldn't hurt me. We went rolling over and over each other in the dirt.

"Ha ha ha ha ha!" All the puppies laughed!

Buttons even laughed a little, demurely, in a ladylike manner.

"Yeah! Action makes every story better!"

The Pit Bull in the yard to our left of Buttons had

been watching, apparently. The Bull Mastiff was out there, too. I couldn't tell if he was watching or not, but at least he wasn't threatening to kill and eat us. Not right now, anyway. That was a plus.

I started thinking on my feet. "You want action, huh?"

"Yeah!" the puppies all said.

"Yes, please!" Buttons said.

"Of course we want action," the Bull Mastiff said. "Everything else is boring!"

I turned slightly so that I was facing all the neighbors who now listened over the dirt alley between our three yards.

"OK! Oreo and I will act out the rest of the story, then."

"Yay!" the puppies said.

"Thank you so much," Buttons said.

"All right!" the Bull Mastiff and the Pitt Bull said at the same time. They looked at each other and butted heads.

I addressed the two of them for a moment.

"By the way, I'm Raffle, and this is my brother, Oreo. What are your names?"

The Bull Mastiff said, "I'm Roy, and this is my brother, Ocho. Now get on with the story, before we get bored!"

I quickly said, "Alright! Alright!" and looked around for a prop. "Oreo, you guard the entrance to the shed."

He looked at me for a sec, and then ran over there like a good soldier.

"We Kaxians came here to Planet Earth to mine jex."

"What's jex?" just about everyone asked at once.

"It's something we find sometimes when we dig in the ground. The next time I smell some, I'll point it out to you."

"OK," they all said.

"The trouble is," I said, running over to where Oreo guarded the shed door, "the Niques followed us here to Planet Earth, to steal our jex."

Imitating how the pesky little Niques try to squeeze by us and get inside our mines, I tried to squeeze by Oreo and get into the shed.

Oreo was a good guard! He stuck his nose in front of my nose, no matter where I tried to nose in and squeeze through.

I continued my story while I tried to get into the shed.

"Wherever we dig for jex, the Niques show up and try to get into our mine, like I'm trying to get into this shed. We guard our mines, just like Oreo is guarding the shed."

"Who are the Niques?" just about everyone asked except Buttons, who was just being polite.

I stopped my assault on the shed and turned to face my audience.

"You see Niques every day. They are the little fiends who mock us and taunt us and generally try to make our lives miserable. Ten of them live right over there."

I pointed with my nose to our neighbor's house.

"They aren't from Earth, either. They come from a different planet, though. We're from Kax, and the aliens that the humans call "little dogs" are from Nique."

Everyone started talking at once, then. Roy and Ocho were comparing notes on all the Niques in the neighborhood and saying how they might have known those little pests were from another world than ours. The puppies were asking a million questions of me, Oreo, their mother, and even of Ocho and Roy.

The puppies' mother was still, though. She stood there, her pretty blue eyes just blinking.

I'd seen that look before, on the faces of my litter mates, whenever the Kaxian memories were coming back to them. I smiled. Soon, she would remember how to speak Kanx, and Oreo would have someone to practice Kanx with besides me.

Oreo hadn't seen the look before, but he recognized her realization for the experience he'd recently had. He ran over to the fence and wagged his tail while he watched Buttons come home to Kax in her own mind.

I stood there overwhelmed for a minute. Besides Roy, Ocho, Buttons, and her puppies, there were our other neighbors: the two Rottweilers. None of us knew their names. Beyond them, we had a whole neighborhood full of Kaxians who didn't know where they were from or that they were part of a larger pack.

Oreo and I had our work cut out for us.

Our humans came outside to play with us, and we got to be loved, more even than we had given love.

Our male human called out, "Oreo! Go get it!" and he threw the ball.

Oreo looked up at him, wagged his tail, and swiftly fetched the ball for his master.

"Good boy, Oreo!" Our master petted his new second best friend.

"Raffle! Your turn! Get it!" He threw the ball for me, too.

I got the ball for my human, and he petted me for bringing it over.

"You're such a good boy, Raffle. Yes. Yes, you are."

Our female human sat down in her outdoor chair then, and extended her arms out to the sides.

We each went to one hand so she could pet us, and she did. She scratched under our collars where we couldn't get to.

Our male human was humming to himself while he made a fire in the outdoor pit. When he sat down, I went to him, and Oreo stayed with her. We both got petted the entire evening, and we have both been petted, played with, and loved every day since then.

Chapter 28: Oreo

"Oreo, what's gotten into you? You can't bite people!"

My human was talking crazy talk again. Of course I could bite people. I had teeth, didn't I?

She was petting me and scratching that itchy spot in the damp fur under my collar. She was also hugging me, and it was so nice.

But she was lecturing, too.

"What gave you the idea to bite people, anyway? You never did that before."

I said, "Before we bonded? Well, no offense, but I didn't care what happened to you then. I was going to run away. Maybe you remember?"

Of course, she didn't understand me. She was still explaining the obvious, but she was not understanding something herself. I now did care about her, and I would give my life to defend her.

She kept lecturing me.

"People have feelings, just like you do. If you bite them, it will hurt them. I don't hurt people, Oreo. My dog can't go around hurting people, either…"

This lecture was getting boring. I lowered my ears to signal she should pet my head. She did, but she kept on lecturing. She thought I was stupid. Oh well.

She had to know I was just trying to protect her.

She must have chosen me because I would make the best defender. Otherwise, why had she chosen a defender dog out of all the dogs the animal shelter brought to the store?

You know how to recognize a defender dog, don't you? We're the first ones to come forward when you approach a litter or any pack of dogs or puppies. When the pack is running together, we're out in front of the alphas, protecting them. We're usually the biggest in the litter.

Yeah, she had to know that, right?

Right.

Don't tell her I said this, but she was the one who was a little stupid. She took chances with her safety that I just could not tolerate, as her bodyguard. She walked awfully close to Kaxians who had no idea they were Kaxians and could easily do her harm. She went for walks after it was dark, when she couldn't see as well as most animals can.

She even petted cats!

I did my best to make sure she stayed safe, but she didn't make it easy.

She fought me every step of the way!

I was perfectly willing to be on the leash when we went out walking. I no longer pulled on it to try and go chase prey. Not too often, anyway. Sometimes a squirrel would dare me to chase it, and I would get so mad I would forget I was on the leash and try to go after it. I was always sorry when this happened, but my urge to chase small prey is strong.

Anyway, so I had agreed to be on a leash.

And to let her lead.

I let her decide where we would go. That's a big deal!

She doesn't have a very good nose. She can't smell where the best trees are to go pee on. I have to kind of show her. I don't really pull on the leash. No. I just tug a little bit toward the good trees. And you know what? Most of the time she's really good about taking me to the good trees.

Oh, you don't know what makes a tree a good one to pee on?

Heh! I forget, your nose isn't very good, either. It can't be if you're a human. Sorry about that.

Well, what makes a tree a good one to pee on is if everyone else has peed there. Yeah! Because that way we can all check each other out without having to wander all over the park. Oh, I've smelled some trees at dog parks that had the scent of more than 100,000 different dogs on them!

Peeing where the most other dogs have peed gives us status. You know how being seen at a popular human hangout gives humans status? Everyone knows that you know where the cool places to hang out are. Well, then you should be able to understand how peeing on the popular tree gives us status. Same thing.

But it's a waste if we just pee on the popular tree right away.

If I did that, then my scent would cover all the other scents before I got a chance to sniff them all. I still could, but it is much easier before my scent is there. It takes us a while to stop and smell that many different scents. Each scent tells us everything about the dog who left it: how old they are, if they're a boy or a girl, what breed they are, what they ate that day, how long ago they were here, if they come here often... It takes me a second to process that much information. That's why we stand there sniffing the tree for so long before we add our scent to the mix.

And the last one to pee there gets the most status. That's why two of us will stand there and pee over each other's pee, vying to be the last one to pee there until you pull us both away with the leash and say, "Come ON!"

Yeah.

Anyway.

I agreed to be on the leash, and I agreed to let her lead, most of the time.

So I figured she should have agreed to let me protect her as we walked around among all those humans out there who might do her harm. There were dogs, I mean Kaxians out there who might do her harm too. Well, and Niques, but really, how much harm could a Nique do?

Being small, Niques couldn't do much physical harm. However, a direct consequence of the Niques meddling in Kaxian and human affairs is that I and others like me grow up not knowing we're Kaxians. Until we know this, we don't get the Kaxian memories that remind us the humans are intelligent creatures, just like us, who need to be respected.

Yeah, the Niques are intelligent, too, but most of them are little meddling brats. What? Yes, I have had friends and pack mates who were Niques. Yes, I know they aren't all that way. OK, yeah, the Niques need to be respected, too.

Until they disrespect me.

And those memories also told me we needed to protect the humans. Or the dog bond told me that. Or both. It was a really strong need that I had.

All I wanted to do really was walk so I was

between her and the nearest threat.

That was it!

She should have gone along with that, am I right?

Like, if there was a big angry Rottweiler coming toward her from the right, I wanted to stand on her right and watch the guy so he didn't get too close to her.

Or if she walked past a territorial German Shepherd who was barking at her, then I wanted to walk behind her and keep my eyes on him so that he would know she was under my protection and he better not try anything.

You see how reasonable I was being?

But she had this crazy idea that I had to walk on her left side at all times. That was stupid enough, but then she got mad at me for being smarter than her and moving into guard position whenever there was a threat. Yeah! She totally did that.

The next time we were out walking, a man came too close to her, like they often did, and I snapped at him. I was just telling him to back off.

I think she realized then that I had not been listening to her lecture about not biting humans.

"No!" she said firmly.

I stopped in my tracks and looked at her to see what she was talking about.

She took a soft but firm hold on my jaw, held it closed, looked into my eyes, and spoke directly to me then.

"Oreo! Don't bite people!"

Oh!

She was ordering me not to bite people!

Why didn't she just order me in the first place? I would have listened to an order.

Those lectures she gives are a waste of time, though. She will never convince me that biting people is a bad idea. The only reason I've stopped being so protective is that she has ordered me to stop being so protective. Orders work on me. Lecturing doesn't.

I kept still and paid attention, hoping she would know I was taking her seriously.

And that she would pet me.

Or give me a treat.

"And Puppy, this is California. Even if you bite to defend me, a judge can order you put to sleep for it."

This was weird.

Now that she knew I wasn't a puppy, she called me Puppy all the time, as if it was my name. But that wasn't the weirdest part.

She was speaking quietly, but her face was all scrunched up as if she was barking at the neighbors for coming too close to the fence. She never did that, but her face looked like she might at any second, except that her voice wasn't working very well.

Her voice was coming out really funny. Not as in "Ha ha ha! I'm laughing at you!" funny. No. I would never laugh at my human now that we're bonded. Now, all I want to do is protect her.

No, her voice, something was wrong with it. I was worried about her. She could barely talk. She kept gasping for breath, too.

I licked her hands to show her I cared and that she didn't need to lecture me anymore. I would be nice to all the humans, if that was what she wanted, I guessed.

So long as they weren't trying to hurt her.

Or steal things from her.

Or come into the humans' den while she was sleeping or not home.

But she was still trying to talk. "I wish you could understand what I was saying. Then you would realize just how serious it would be if you bit anyone, even someone who meant me harm. It might mean I would lose you, Oreo. I can't lose you now. Not when we're finally getting along."

Now water was running out of her eyes!

I'm not kidding!

Her eyes were leaking!

It was the weirdest thing.

I looked her in the eye and wagged my tail while licking her hands, trying to show her I did understand what she was saying, and I would be good for her. I didn't want to leave her anymore. I needed her to know that.

But I wasn't going to promise never to bite.

No, hear me out.

Now that we were bonded, I felt the need to protect her from harm. She was all choked up over how losing me would make her sad. Well, she must not have stopped to think how losing *her* would make *me* feel sad.

I'm a defender, and what I do is defend her.
***

This is the end of Dog Aliens 2.

Raffle and Oreo are now brothers in spirit, not just in name. The fun will continue sometime in 2014. Sign up for the Dog Aliens mailing list at the author's blog to be notified when you can get

Dog Aliens 3: She Wolf Neya

http://size12bystpatricksday.blogspot.com/

Made in the USA
Charleston, SC
03 March 2014